NIGHT
OF THE
BAYONETS

NIGHT OF THE BAYONETS

The Texel Uprising and Hitler's Revenge,
April–May 1945

ERIC LEE

Greenhill Books

Night of the Bayonets
First published in 2020 by
Greenhill Books,
c/o Pen & Sword Books Ltd,
47 Church Street, Barnsley,
S. Yorkshire, S70 2AS

www.greenhillbooks.com
contact@greenhillbooks.com

ISBN: 978-1-78438-468-5

All rights reserved.
© Eric Lee, 2020

The right of Eric Lee to be identified as author of this work has been asserted in accordance with Section 77 of the Copyrights Designs and Patents Act 1988.

CIP data records for this title are available from the British Library

Designed and typeset by Donald Sommerville

Printed and bound in the UK by TJ International Ltd, Padstow

Typeset in 11.8/16 pt Arno Pro Regular

For Cindy Berman

Contents

	List of Plates	ix
	Prologue	xi
	Introduction	xiii
Chapter 1	Georgia and the Georgians	1
Chapter 2	Barbarossa	18
Chapter 3	The Exiles	27
Chapter 4	Sonderverband *Bergmann*	35
Chapter 5	Recruiting the Georgians	43
Chapter 6	Unreliable Allies	50
Chapter 7	Texel in Wartime	59
Chapter 8	The Georgians and the Dutch	66
Chapter 9	Day of Birth	79
Chapter 10	The German Counter-Attack	95
Chapter 11	Hunters and Hunted	109
Chapter 12	Where Were the Allies?	124
Chapter 13	Liberation	127
Chapter 14	Back in the USSR	142
Chapter 15	The Making of a Myth	147
Chapter 16	Crucified Island	157
Chapter 17	'A Country of Heroes'	164
Chapter 18	Justice	172
Chapter 19	An Accounting	175
Epilogue	In the 'Russian Cemetery'	186
Appendix	Counting the Losses	189
	Acknowledgements	191
	Notes	192
	Bibliography	200
	General Index	202
	Index of Names	204

Plates

The swastika flag flying over Den Burg, Texel's main town.
Aeronautical and War Museum Texel (LOMT)
One of the German bunkers on the island. *Author*
Indian soldiers serving in the Wehrmacht. *(LOMT)*
The Hotel de Lindeboom, HQ of the German occupation forces.
LOMT
A German soldier on Texel fraternising with local women. *LOMT*
German soldiers enjoying a beer. *LOMT*
A German soldier having a snooze on the peaceful island. *LOMT*
German personnel queuing for rations. *LOMT*
German troops playing games on Texel. *LOMT*
Members of the Georgian Legion. *LOMT*
Georgians of the 822nd Battalion relaxing. *LOMT*
Local Dutch Nazis. *LOMT*
Shalva Loladze, leader of the uprising. *Wikipedia*
Two wounded Georgian soldiers. *Wikipedia*
The bloodstained map used by Shalva Loladze. *Author*
The old lighthouse on Texel. *Author*
The Georgian Military Cemetery. *Author*
Poster for the Soviet film *Crucified Island*.
Memorial for Cornelia Boon-Verberg. *Author*
The grave of Evgeni Artemidze. *Author*

Prologue

At 2 a. m. on 10 April 1945, Howard Dawes and Reg Earl, coastguards posted to the tiny village of Mundesley in Norfolk were surprised by the sight of a bright flare fired from a small lifeboat approaching out of the North Sea.[1]

The boat was painted in white and flew the flag of the Red Cross. A Royal Air Force reconnaissance plane responded to the boat's flares, and guided it to the coast.

According to local historian David Brandon, 'It was clear they intended to land ... The Home Guard was alerted and they mustered on the beach, rifles at the ready, determined to give the enemy a good drubbing.'[2] But the men who landed turned out not to be the enemy at all.

When the boat reached the shore it offloaded a most unusual crew. Ten of the men were Dutch. They had travelled for some twenty-four hours and told the startled British that they came from Texel, the largest of the Wadden Islands off the Dutch coast. But four of the men on board were not Dutch and were wearing German uniforms.[3]

As one of the Dutch men later recalled,

> I waded to the shore to meet two members of the coast guard. They offered me a cigarette before they said anything. We went ashore, but two people stayed behind to guard the boat. We were wet, nervous, and tired, but were welcomed with big mugs of tea. We were given dry clothes from the military post and a warm bed. Two hours later, I was woken up by a man from Scotland Yard (Police) who started to question me. I had a written request for military help with me. He agreed to pass

it on to the Dutch and English governments immediately. This eased my mind because it was clear that the situation on Texel was rapidly becoming untenable.⁴

The Dutch men were then dressed in military uniforms and travelled by train to London the next day. After a few days, they were invited to an audience with the exiled Queen Wilhelmina. The Queen made the men feel welcome. One of them later recalled,

> After a while, she asked if I would mind taking a walk with her in the garden to tell the whole story about the Texel tragedy... The Queen's eyes filled up with tears. It appeared that the Queen knew much about the events in Holland.⁵

Meanwhile, the four men who had been wearing German uniforms were whisked off for interrogation. They were taken to Kempton Park racecourse, south-west of London, which had been turned into a facility to process incoming German prisoners of war. The horse stables were made into temporary sleeping quarters for the prisoners, 120 of whom could be processed at any time. There were three interrogation rooms which had been suites from where the rich and famous had watched the horse races in the days before the war.⁶

It quickly turned out that the 'German soldiers' were not German at all, but were in fact former Red Army men from Soviet Georgia. Years earlier they had surrendered to the Germans and had subsequently been recruited into the Georgian Legion, a part of the German Army. That explained the German uniforms.

The story they told was extraordinary.

Introduction

This book tells the story of the final battle of the Second World War in Europe. That battle began on 6 April 1945 on the small Dutch island of Texel. It did not end until the arrival of Canadian troops on 20 May – which was more than two weeks *after* the surrender of the German forces in the Netherlands.

The soldiers on both sides of the battle wore the same uniforms. On the one side were Georgians who had for the most part been Soviet soldiers who were captured in battle, then, when taken to German prisoner of war camps, they had been offered the opportunity to sign up to the German side. Those Georgian soldiers on Texel were part of the 822nd Eastern Battalion of the Wehrmacht. Fighting against them on Texel were German soldiers who until the early morning hours of 6 April believed their Georgian colleagues to be loyal comrades. And caught between them were the Dutch, who initially believed that their island had been liberated by the Allies, but later found themselves stuck in the middle of a bloody battle in which dozens of civilians, including children, lost their lives. It is an extraordinary tale, not least for the fact that the German surrender on 5 May did nothing to end the fighting on the island.

While the story of the Georgian uprising on Texel is little-known to most people, it not an 'unknown battle'. In both Georgia and the Netherlands, books have been published and documentary films released. There was even a full length Soviet feature film made about it. (More about that later.) But it remains largely an unknown story outside those two countries. And, as we shall also see, the history that is 'known' is not all true and the creation of the myth of Texel over the course of several decades is itself an important part of this story.

This book begins, as it must, in Georgia. That country has a history spanning thousands of years, but I want to write about the period beginning roughly around the First World War. That was a time when Georgians, Russians and Germans interacted, providing a basis for the later friendship between some Georgians and Germans, and for a more complex relationship with Russia. The Germans and Georgians during the Second World War were inspired in part by things they did in the First, including the formation of a Georgian Legion as part of the German Army. The 822nd Battalion was a part of that Georgian Legion. And of course some people lived long enough to participate in both world wars.

It's also important to go back a few years in the history of the Netherlands, as it turned out that the Georgian rebels on Texel had been talking to, and were influenced by, leading figures in the Dutch Communist Party. The involvement of the Dutch Communists in the decision of the Georgians to rebel, and to rebel when they did, has been the subject of some controversy. Their history, and in particular the period of the Hitler–Stalin Pact (1939–41), deserves our attention as it may explain why some of the Dutch Communists were so enthusiastic about the Georgian rebels on Texel – both during and after the war.

The German invasion of the Soviet Union on 22 June 1941 set the stage for the story I will tell in this book. It is therefore necessary to look into the fate of the millions of Soviet soldiers, Georgians and others, who fell into German captivity. How some of them were persuaded to join the German Army is discussed. In the course of my research I came upon the intriguing story of Sonderverband *Bergmann*, an élite German force full of Georgians and other Caucasians, which was a forerunner of the Georgian Legion.

The Germans, and in particular Hitler himself, never fully trusted the former Soviet soldiers who in captivity agreed to join the German side. Their suspicions proved to be well-founded, for at a later point in the war, when it was clear that the Germans were going to lose, there were several incidents of Georgians and other *Osttruppen* ('Eastern Troops') turning on their German masters.

The unreliability of the Georgians and others, and the fact that there were numerous cases of them defecting back to the Soviet ranks, led the

Wehrmacht to take the decision to deploy them to the West. That's how men from the foothills of the Caucasus found themselves patrolling the flat fields of the Dutch Wadden Islands.

The story of the rebellion itself can be told through many eyes. We have the post-war interviews given by the former German commander in which he blasts the Georgians for their treason. The Georgians themselves, those who survived, were able to tell their stories, too. In the Netherlands, there have been books and documentary films in which the residents of Texel told the tale of the uprising as they understood it. There are the records of the time held by the British military, mostly intercepts of German radio messages which were decrypted by the teams at Bletchley Park. There is the eyewitness account taken down in real time by British interrogators of the four Georgians who landed that night at Mundesley, on the Norfolk coast.

In telling the story of the battle, I wanted also to give a full account of what happened next. The survival of hundreds of the Georgians, and their fate in the Soviet Union later, is not something that could easily have been predicted. A big part of what happened next was the creation of the myth of Texel. What was striking to me was the persistence of the myth in Georgia itself long after the Communist period was over and the Soviet Union was only a memory.

One cannot tell a story like this, I think, without trying to give a moral accounting, to attempt to understand who was to blame for a tragedy that took so many lives, including many innocent lives of civilians. Were the Germans responsible? Were the Georgians?

The story of the Georgian uprising on Texel is above all the story of the people who were there. Those people were Georgians, Germans, Dutch and, much later, Canadians.

In the chapters to come, you'll meet the dashing Shalva Loladze, a former Red Air Force pilot and the highest-ranking Georgian officer on Texel. He is joined by Evgeni Artemidze who, with his bushy moustache and self-confidence, became known to the local civilians as 'Little Stalin'. He famously summed up his war by saying that while he wore the uniform of Hitler, his heart belonged to Stalin. Grisha Baindurashvili was one of the Georgian Texel survivors who was able to describe his terrifying face-to-face confrontation with a German soldier in the final days of the war. And then there's General Shalva Maglakelidze, former commander of the Georgian Legion, who survived the war but was kidnapped from West Germany and taken back to the Soviet Union to a most surprising fate.

Among the Germans, we'll meet Dr Theodor Oberländer, whose Sonderverband *Bergmann* was a forerunner of the Georgian Legion, and who had a successful political career in post-war Germany until his wartime activities were exposed. Major Klaus Breitner, the commander of the 822nd Battalion on Texel, was supposed to have been killed on the very first night of the rebellion, but as we shall see he was not where he was expected to be – and he therefore lived to tell the tale. Heinz Hlawatschek was the first German to set foot on Texel and, unlike the others, he was a consistent supporter of the Dutch resistance, providing them with considerable help during the war. And we'll hear the testimony of one of the many German soldiers who were deployed to Texel after the rebellion had broken out to carry out Hitler's order to 'kill all the Georgians'.

The people of Texel will tell their story in their own words, and among the more memorable characters is a young boy, Hans Verhoeven, who was sent to the island to keep him safe – and then found himself in the thick of battle. His memoir, written many years after the war, makes for gripping reading. The Dutch resistance leader Jacob Keijzer, who posed as a fascist sympathiser for much of the war, remembered his first clandestine meetings with the Georgians – and his suspicions about them. And we'll meet some of the Dutch Communists who came into contact with the Georgians in the months running up to their rebellion, among them a woman whom they came to call their 'mother', and a Communist underground leader on the mainland who some today accuse of encouraging a rebellion that could only end in tragedy.

Finally, the Canadians will arrive on the scene, led by Lt.-Col. William Douglas Kirk, a distinguished officer who had come over to Europe to fight on the very first ship after the outbreak of war in 1939. We have eyewitness reports from two of the soldiers who served under his command, describing what they saw and how they felt about it many years later. And we'll meet the high-ranking Canadian officer whose father wrote best-selling spy fiction, but who found the birds of Texel far more interesting than the Georgians he was sent to escort home.

The story of the Georgian uprising on Texel is of course little more than a footnote in the history of the Second World War. At the same time that it was happening, bloody battles were being fought across Europe, including in the Reich capital Berlin. Part of the reason why the Canadians arrived on the scene so late was because Texel was so far removed from the front lines where most of the fighting was taking place during those final weeks of the war.

Its significance, as we shall see, lies in the fact that the Georgian soldiers serving there, thousands of miles from their homes, were crushed between two monstrous totalitarian regimes. Whether they wore Hitler's uniform but gave their heart to Stalin, as Evgeni Artemidze put it, or not, they rose up on that night, choosing a path that would send most of them to early graves. And they did it for the same reason that they first agreed to wear the uniform of the Wehrmacht or, earlier, to raise their hands and surrender to the Germans.

They were young men who were simply trying to survive the war and get home.

Chapter 1

Georgia and the Georgians

To this day, the uprising which took place on Texel in April–May 1945 is known as *De Russenoorlog* (the Russian War) to the Dutch. The cemetery where the Georgian soldiers are now buried was long known as the 'Russian cemetery'. Even the British interrogators who interviewed the four men who landed in Mundesley that morning in April 1945 referred to them as 'Russians'. But they were not Russians. And that matters because, being Georgians, they had taken an almost unbelievable journey from their homeland which ended in them wearing German uniforms, and landing on the Norfolk coast with a story to tell.

Georgia is a small country situated to the south of the Caucasus mountains, on the Black Sea coast. For centuries it was surrounded by various empires – the Persians, the Ottomans, the Russians – which would, from time to time, invade it. For long periods Georgia had its independent kingdoms too.

It is a stunningly beautiful country, and includes some of the highest mountains in Europe, as it sits astride the Caucasus range. Its climate is radically different from that of Russia to its north, parts of the country being sub-tropical. In both tsarist and Soviet times, Georgia served as a playground for the Russian élites. It was the source not only of many of the empire's best fruits and vegetables, but also of the legendary Georgian wine. Georgians claim to have been making wine for some 8,000 years, and have their own unique way to make it. They use large earthenware vessels called *kvevri* to ferment, store and age the wine. Their language bears little resemblance to Russian and doesn't use Cyrillic (or Latin) characters. Georgian has its own script.

For all those reasons, calling Georgians 'Russians' is inaccurate, to say the least, but as we shall see, pretty much everyone in our story did so.

In July 1783, Georgian independence came to an end with the Treaty of Georgievsk (signed by Catherine II the Great of Russia and Erekle II of Kartalinia-Kakhetia, in eastern Georgia). This turned Georgia into a protectorate of the powerful Russian Empire. By 1801, Georgia was an integral part of that empire. The result of this was that Russia gained access to the Turkish frontier and to port cities like Batumi on the Black Sea coast. Russia in tsarist times (as in the Soviet period) was an expansionist power, with its eyes on Constantinople. Georgia was first an obstacle, and then a stepping stone toward those Russian goals.

Georgia and Russia were both historically Christian countries, and Georgia needed protection from the powerful Muslim states on its southern frontier. Though Georgia lost its independence in 1801, it gained more than a century of relative peace and stability under the protection of the Russian tsar. But that stability came at a cost. Georgia was increasingly Russified, with its own language, culture and church given second-class status. As a result, there were increasing numbers of Georgians who longed for a restoration of national independence. These included important literary figures like Ilya Chavchavadze, a poet and political leader who was murdered in September 1907. To this day, no one knows who killed him – though Stalin and the few Georgian Bolsheviks of the time have been blamed by some.

Most Georgians seemed to be content to retain links with Russia. Even the Social Democrats, who by the beginning of the twentieth century had emerged as the largest political force in the country, had little interest in Georgian independence. They saw themselves as members of a *Russian* political party, one which would some day overthrow the tsarist regime and establish a democratic federal republic. After the revolution, perhaps, Georgia would get a measure of autonomy. In the end, Georgia got more than that – and the Social Democrats became the proud leaders of a *Georgian* republic.

Their party was unique among the new Social Democratic parties that were springing up around the world at that time. Those parties, the British Labour Party among them, were overwhelmingly based on a combination of industrial workers and intellectuals. But Georgia was a poor country and had a very small industrial working class. It remained a largely agrarian society. In the course of a peasant rebellion in the western Georgian province of Guria, which began in 1904, the Georgian Social Democrats played a leadership role, and eventually admitted many of the rebellious peasants as party members. As a result, the Social Democrats became a mass political force, much larger than any other party in Georgia.

Several of the Georgian Social Democrat leaders became prominent figures in the Russian state *duma*, the country's parliament, in the late tsarist period. When the Social Democratic Party split, with Lenin leading the hard-line Bolshevik faction, his opponents – who were more firmly part of the Western European democratic tradition – became known as Mensheviks. The Georgian Social Democrats were almost all Mensheviks. Only one well-known Georgian took Lenin's side – Iosif Dzhugashvili, better known as Stalin.

The Georgian Legion in the First World War

The Georgians who landed on the Norfolk coast in April 1945 were serving in the Georgian Legion, part of the German Army. That Legion took its name and its inspiration from a Georgian Legion which had been a part of the German Army in the First World War.

During the four years leading up to Georgian independence from the tsarist Russian Empire in May 1918, the country was on the very front lines of the First World War, as the Russian Army battled the Turks. When the war began in the summer of 1914, a 'Germanophile mood dominated in Georgia' according to Noe Zhordania, the leader of the Social Democrats.[1] Zhordania would go on to become the head of government of independent Georgia and continued to lead the country's government-in-exile for many years to come. Though he acknowledged the 'Germanophile mood' in the country, he didn't share it.

Zhordania and the future foreign minister of independent Georgia, Akaki Chkhenkeli, expressed sympathy for the Allied cause, as did a number of Russian Social Democrats, among them Georgi Plekhanov, the founding father of Russian Marxism. This may have had something to do with their general orientation towards Western European ideas of democracy, and their lack of interest in securing independence for

Georgia. But others in Georgia saw Imperial Germany as an ally in the fight to break free from the tsarist regime – and this view of Germany as the country that would help to free Georgia from Russia persisted for decades afterwards.

Count Friedrich Werner von der Schulenburg, a former German vice-consul in Tbilisi, the Georgian capital (then known as Tiflis), founded a Georgian Legion in 1915 while serving as a German officer attached to the Turkish Army. With the backing of the Berlin-based 'Committee of Independent Georgia' Schulenburg pulled together a force of several thousand men, despite the opposition of the Georgian Social Democrats. The Legion's commander was a German, Horst Schliephack. The top Georgian officer was Leo Kereselidze.

The Legion was based in Turkey throughout the war and didn't get much of a chance to fight. The Germans had hoped to use the Georgians to incite rebellion inside the Russian Empire, believing that smaller nations like Georgia would be keen to break free of the tsarist yoke. But the Turks did not share this vision, and saw the soldiers of the Georgian Legion as just another unit of their vast army. Relations between the Georgian Legion and the Turkish government were never good. The Legion sat out most of the war not far from the Black Sea coast, and was never sent into combat against the Russian Army.

In January 1917, with the war still raging, the Legion was dissolved – just in time for some of its officers to return to Georgia following the revolution which began in the imperial capital, Petrograd, and which brought an end to the tsarist regime across the Russian Empire.

There are many differences between the Georgian Legion of the First World War and that of the Second – largely due to the fact that the Germany which fought Russia in 1914–18 was not the Nazi Germany of the Second World War. No one in Georgia seemed to have any problem with men who volunteered for the Georgian Legion during the First World War, as they were not tainted with the criminal aspects of the Nazi regime. Returning veterans of the Georgian Legion in 1917 were welcomed back and played a role in the formation of the new Georgian national army.

Georgia Becomes Independent

The Georgian Social Democrats played key roles in the revolution that erupted in March 1917 in Petrograd. One of them, Karlo Chkheidze, was elected head of the Petrograd Soviet of Workers and Peasants Deputies, which was effectively governing the city. Another, Irakli Tsereteli, later became a minister in Alexander Kerensky's provisional government.

Back in Georgia, the local Social Democratic leaders, most notably Noe Zhordania, had power fall into their hands as the old regime faded away. This was literally the case; the tsarist official in charge of the whole Transcaucasian region packed his bags and fled, at the last moment inviting the Georgian Social Democrats to take power. But they had little interest in Georgian independence and were content to see the country remain a part of the democratic federal republic that seemed to be coming to replace the old Russian Empire.

But this was not to be. Vladimir Lenin and the Bolsheviks he led seized power in a *coup d'état* in Petrograd in November 1917. Elections were then held across the empire to choose a Constituent Assembly which would draft a new constitution. The Bolsheviks did poorly in those elections, and soldiers loyal to the government of Lenin and Leon Trotsky dispersed the first meeting of the assembly, in which the Bolsheviks were a minority, in January 1918. Instead of the long-awaited democratic federal republic, the Bolsheviks established a one-party state across most of the former empire. The Georgian Social Democrats, including Chkheidze and Tsereteli, who had played such prominent roles in the early months of the Russian Revolution, were forced to flee home to Georgia.

Back in Georgia, Zhordania and his comrades had no interest in living under Lenin's dictatorship, and by April 1918, together with the neighbouring countries of Armenia and Azerbaijan, they formed a Transcaucasian Federation, independent of Russia. But this federation did not last. Under the pressure of a resurgent Turkish military bent on biting off chunks of the old Russian provinces, the federation broke apart. Heeding the advice of German Army officers with whom the Georgians had been negotiating, on 26 May 1918 the Georgians proclaimed independence.

The newly independent Georgian republic found itself sharing a border with Turkey, with no Russian army to speak of standing between the two countries. What remained of that army, now a hungry and undisciplined mass, was engaged in a disorderly retreat through Georgia. The presence of that army on Georgian soil became a security problem of not inconsiderable magnitude.

Other security problems were to arise later on, including a border dispute with Armenia and a growing threat from the north as Russian armies (both White and Red) cast their hungry eyes over the three breakaway Transcaucasian republics. In early 1918, the Turkish Army was on the march and it posed the gravest threat to Georgian independence. The Georgians, lacking a powerful military of their own, needed a protector who could help the new republic stave off the Turks. The most suitable candidate for that role seemed to be Germany.

The Georgians also needed to reach agreement with the Germans following the disastrous Brest-Litovsk peace treaty signed by the Soviet government. In addition to giving away vast swathes of Russian territory, including Ukraine, to the Germans, the Bolsheviks also signed away large chunks of Georgian territory to the Turks. The Georgians had no say in any of this and Brest-Litovsk was one more reason the Georgians were now ready to part ways with Russia.

The Germans, meanwhile, had interests of their own in the region. Though the war would end within six months, Germany in May 1918 was not yet a defeated power. It still had the strength to launch offensives on the Western Front, and its armies had decisively defeated the Russians. In June 1918 German artillery bombarded Paris; the oil-rich city of Baku fell to the German-allied Turks in September. The war was not yet over by any means.

Germany desperately needed oil from Azerbaijan and metals to help in steel production, which Georgia produced in abundance. As historian Donald Rayfield wrote, 'For Germany in 1918, access to Georgia was a matter of life and death.'[2]

General Erich Ludendorff later wrote about why he supported German forces occupying Georgia. This was primarily in order to acquire both raw materials from Georgia and oil from Azerbaijan, he said. Even though Germany hardly had the troops to spare in the middle of a world war, Ludendorff felt that Turkey was not a reliable ally. 'That we could not rely on Turkey in this matter had been once again demonstrated by her conduct in Batum,' he wrote, referring to the Georgian port. The Turks 'claimed the right to retain all the stocks for' themselves, he complained. 'We could expect to get oil from Baku only if we helped ourselves.'[3]

Negotiations with the Germans began even before Georgia was an independent state. These talks were closely linked to the negotiations with Turkey to end the war on the Caucasian front.

On 26 May 1918, the day that the Transcaucasian Federation broke apart and Georgia declared its independence, it faced an ultimatum from Turkey which demanded even more territory than the Bolsheviks had conceded at Brest-Litovsk. Now was the time to quickly reach a deal with the Germans to pre-empt their Turkish allies before they moved to seize even more Georgian territory.

Field Marshal von Hindenburg and General Ludendorff, by this time effectively Germany's rulers, ordered Freiherr Friedrich Kress von Kressenstein, a Bavarian general, to head a military mission to Georgia. In addition to access to Georgia's raw materials and Baku's oil, Ludendorff hoped Georgia could be used by the Germans for an eventual attack on British India.

The Turks were impatient, and they forced Georgia to capitulate in Batumi. The German officers coming in from the Black Sea were forced to land further north, in Poti, to avoid falling into the hands of their Turkish allies. They protested to the Turks that they had gone too far, overstepping the Brest-Litovsk treaty.

The Georgian diplomats who had been meeting with the Turks now reached a separate agreement with Germany, unknown to the Turks, which was signed by the Georgian foreign minister Chkhenkeli and the German General Otto von Lossow on a ship, the *Minna Horn*, in Poti. General von Lossow confided to the Georgians that Turkey and Soviet Russia were on the brink of concluding a secret pact, which would have been a disaster for the small country wedged between them.

The first document the Georgians and Germans signed recognised the Brest-Litovsk agreement. The Georgian Social Democrats had been furious at the Russian Bolsheviks for signing away their territory without even asking their opinion. But in the meantime, the facts on the ground had changed. The Germans and Turks were in a far better bargaining position, and without an intact Russian army to hold them at bay, the Georgians had no choice but to agree to the Brest-Litovsk terms.

That agreement also gave the Germans the right to use the Georgian railroads until the end of the war. Use of the railroad was essential if Germany was to extract manganese and other raw materials from the country. There were other economic parts of the new agreement too. A Georgian–German Mining Joint Stock Company was set up with equal rights and shares for both countries. The Germans were given the right to purchase all excess output from Georgia's mines and to regulate the country's naval communications. Germany's currency, the mark, was to be legal tender in Georgia. Most of these concessions proved to be theoretical, as their implementation was thwarted by the sudden end of the war and Germany's defeat in November 1918.

In exchange for those concessions, the Germans agreed to help mediate between Georgia and Turkey. This was quickly accomplished with the signing of an agreement on 4 June 1918 between the new Georgian Prime Minister, Noe Ramishvili, and the Turks in which the latter formally recognised the Georgian state.

Immediately after signing the agreement with the Germans, foreign minister Chkhenkeli travelled to Berlin together with a delegation of Georgians. They remained in the German capital for several months. There they proposed bringing Georgia under German protection as a 'dominion' of the German Reich, but apparently the Kaiser vetoed this idea.

We don't know what would have happened had Germany won the war; perhaps a German protectorate would have been established eventually. It is also not clear how the German government viewed a country ruled by Social Democrats, as many of the German Social Democrats were alleged to have been 'disloyal' to their country during the world war.

Years later, Trotsky sought to explain the decision of the Georgian Social Democrats to make a deal with the German imperialists. It was not enough for Trotsky to oppose their decision, to accuse them of betraying the working class and colluding with imperialism. Trotsky also needed to explain *why* the Georgian Social Democrats reached out to the German imperialists. In his view, it had nothing to do with Germany's need for Georgia's manganese or Baku's oil, nor did it have anything to do with Georgia's desire for a protector against the Turks. Instead, he insisted, 'The German troops were brought into Georgia, as into Finland, the Baltic countries and the Ukraine, chiefly against the Bolsheviks.'[4]

The Georgian Bolsheviks, who in 1918 and for years afterwards were a tiny, ineffectual group with hardly any influence in their country, were, in Trotsky's view, the real reason behind the Georgian–German alliance. Having exposed the 'real reason' behind the deal with Germany, Trotsky berated the Georgians for hypocrisy:

> When they held the posts of Ministers in an All-Russian government, the Georgian Mensheviks accused us of being in alliance with the German General Staff, and through the Tsarist courts charged us with high treason. They declared that the Brest-Litovsk Peace, which opened 'the gates of the revolution' to German imperialism, was a betrayal of Russia. It was precisely with this cry that they called for the overthrow of the Bolsheviks, and, when the revolution became too hot for them, split Trans-Caucasia away from Russia, and later Georgia from Trans-Caucasia, thereby really opening wide the gates of 'democracy' for the troops of the Kaiser.[5]

While some of this is nonsense, Trotsky had a point about Brest-Litovsk. The Georgians, and indeed all three Transcaucasian republics, had felt betrayed by the Russians for their concessions to the Germans at Brest-Litovsk. To come back just a couple of months later and agree to the very same concessions does seem, on the face of it, to be a bit unfair. But only on the surface. In reality, the defeated Russians were in a position of relative strength when negotiating at Brest-Litovsk, compared to where things stood just a few months later. By June 1918, with almost nothing standing between the Turkish Army and Tbilisi, Brest-Litovsk was starting to look like a good deal to the Georgians.

Trotsky's description of the German occupation of Georgia became a part of Soviet-era history, lasting long after his fall from power, his exile and eventual murder at the hands of Stalin. This is the view that was taught to Georgians during the seven decades of Soviet rule. Trotsky rejected the idea that Georgia invited the Germans to help protect the country against the Turks. He wrote:

> The role of the German troops in the border states of Russia during 1918 was quite definite. In Finland they acted as the executioners of the workers' revolution, in the Baltic states they did the same. They passed through the whole of the Ukraine, breaking up the Soviets, massacring the Communists, and disarming the workers and peasants. [Zhordania] had no reason to expect that they would enter Georgia with any other aim. But it was precisely for this reason that the Menshevik government invited the troops of the indomitable Hohenzollerns – that as against the Turkish troops they had all the advantage of discipline.[6]

The Georgia Trotsky described was one in which the Social Democratic government was faced by constant unrest, with peasant uprisings, worker rebellions, and so on, and with a powerful Georgian Bolshevik party ready at any moment to seize power on behalf of the working class, as they did in Russia. Without the Germans around, Trotsky was convinced, the Social Democrats would have soon lost their grasp on power – and not to the Turks, but to the Bolsheviks:

> One can ... state quite confidently that in spite of the White terror, supplemented by paper flowers of rhetoric, the Menshevik dictatorship would have been swept away, without leaving a trace, by the rapid current of the revolutionary movement, had it not been for the presence of foreign troops in the country. It was not the German Marx that helped the Mensheviks to maintain themselves through that period, but the German Von Kress.

In the Russian Bolshevik view, which during Soviet times became the accepted history of the country, the Georgian Social Democrats were solely concerned with crushing the Bolsheviks, and faced no other threats of any significance, such as Turkey or even General Denikin's White armies, which dominated southern Russia at that time.

Zhordania, according to Trotsky, would have expected those German troops to break up soviets, disarm the workers, and massacre Communists. But the Social Democrats actually controlled the soviets, in which they had large majorities, and there was no need for the Germans to break these up. The idea that the Germans might disarm the Georgian workers made no sense, as the armed proletarians of the People's Guard were fanatically loyal to the Social Democratic government. The soviets were not broken up, the workers were not disarmed, and the repression of Georgia's tiny and ineffectual Communist Party was done entirely by the Georgian police and People's Guard, without any need for German help.

An alternative view, and a more accurate one, of how the Georgians and Germans came to be partners for a few months in 1918 was given by Karl Kautsky, who visited Georgia for several months at the end of 1920. Kautsky was a leading figure in the international Social Democratic movement, having written several of its key texts and serving as the literary executor of Karl Marx's estate. Kautsky began with a longer historical view, noting that, 'The Germans have been popular in Georgia for a long time, thanks to the Wurtemberg colonists who settled there a hundred years ago, as peasants, and retained their nationality until today, earning for themselves a good reputation.'

It was not only the German colonists who made the Georgians amenable to the German occupiers. To the Georgian Social Democrats, Germany was the land of Marx, Engels, Lasalle, Bebel and Liebknecht. It was the heartland of Social Democracy, with the most powerful Social Democratic party in the world and the strongest trade unions.

Kautsky, though a life-long opponent of the Kaiser's regime, supported the Georgian decision to turn toward Germany for protection in 1918. The Germans, he wrote,

> came to Georgia not as plunderers but as organisers of its productive forces, as they needed the Georgian products, especially manganese, and also its railways. Thus they brought

to Georgia precisely what was most lacking in the country, and what it could only obtain speedily by foreign assistance, namely economic organisation.

The deal made between Germany and Georgia forced the Russian Bolsheviks to sign an amendment to the Brest-Litovsk treaty on 27 August 1918. It stipulated that Russia consented to Germany's recognition of Georgian independence. In a sense, this meant Russian recognition of Georgia's independence too, though this would not become formal until the Georgian–Russian peace treaty in May 1920. This was not necessarily a massive concession by the Soviets, as Lenin had already acknowledged the right of the border states of the Russian Empire to secede, and had accepted this in the case of Finland, Poland and the three Baltic republics.

German troops arrived in Tbilisi just two weeks after Georgia had proclaimed independence and were welcomed as protectors from the Turks. Three days after their arrival the Social Democratic government issued a declaration, informing the population that those troops were there by invitation 'for the purpose of defending the frontiers' of the country. The Workers' and Soldiers' Soviet in Tbilisi backed the government on this.

Within a month, the Germans had taken control of the country's ports and railways from the hands of the Turks. They began work on exporting hundreds of thousands of tons of manganese from the mines in Chiatura to Germany. They lent 54 million Deutschmarks (at a very high rate of interest) in order to back the new Georgian currency. They began planning to develop the port of Poti, to lay a cable under the Black Sea and to build an oil pipeline from Batumi to Poti.

But all did not go smoothly, despite the Georgian government's commitment to developing the friendship. The Georgian workers, who unlike their comrades in Russia under Lenin, belonged to free and independent trade unions with the right to strike, had other ideas. According to Donald Rayfield,

> On 27 June the first consignment of manganese left Poti for Germany, but the shortage of dockers, and the undernourished,

strike-prone state of those that did work, left more manganese behind than could ever be shipped. Similar blockages prevented the export of Abkhaz tobacco, highland wool and Kakhetian copper, or the import of much-needed flour.

The Germans were furious. They were no more tolerant of striking workers than were the Bolsheviks. Kress demanded that the Georgian Social Democrats crack down on the workers. One imagines that if the Germans had remained in Georgia after 1918, they may have lost patience with the country's militant workers, and possibly with its Social Democratic government as well.

The Germans also called on Georgia to integrate its army with the armed workers of the People's Guard and to denationalise lands seized from the nobles. They called on the government to deport several thousand stranded Russian soldiers to the Crimea where they could join the White armies in the fight against the Bolsheviks, and in general wanted Georgia to abandon neutrality and to help overthrow the Russian Bolsheviks. The Georgians would have none of it.

There were even attempts by the Germans to see if the old Georgian monarchy could be revived. According to a Georgian propaganda pamphlet from 1919, 'Germany tried, in vain, to impose one of her Princes as ruler of the country, but it failed against the Socialistic majority, which presented a solid democratic front to the schemes of Germany.'

Meanwhile, the German occupiers were busy with other things as well. They offered scholarships to attend German universities and established a German school in Tbilisi. They also revived a German-language newspaper that was quite anti-socialist, *Die kaukasische Post*. Its influence would no doubt have been limited both by the small number of German-speakers in Georgia and by the equally small number of anti-socialists.

Just five months after German troops entered Tbilisi, the world war ended with a German defeat. The German soldiers in Georgia, who had previously been so well-behaved and therefore welcomed by most Georgians, 'became an undisciplined rabble'. In early December 1918 the first British troops arrived, among them some Indian soldiers. The

German military headquarters in the Palace Hotel was burned down. Before the year was over, German forces began withdrawing from the Georgian capital.

Early in the new year, the Georgian government held a welcoming banquet for the British military mission. But at the very same time, the war minister also gave General Kress a farewell dinner. The Georgians were sad to see the Germans go, and not at all happy to be replacing them with the British. Kress and his men remained in Georgia until February, and were treated by the British as prisoners of war.

The Georgian Social Democrats were, if anything, practical men. Facing the imminent threat of Turkish invasion, and a possible Turkish-Soviet pact, they engineered a deal with Germany that guaranteed the country's borders and provided a measure of internal stability. Kautsky wrote that 'The German occupation was raised by the achievement of troops in occupation. Georgia is one of the few countries in this war where the German Armies have done propaganda work for Germany.' (One wonders which were the others.)

Donald Rayfield insisted that 'There is no doubt that, by stiffening the administration and forming a regular army, in autumn 1918 the German military mission saved Georgia from internal chaos and from Turkish invasion and Armenian encroachments.' The Germans played a small role in assisting the Georgians in the first days of their short conflict with Armenia at the end of the year.

When the Germans left Georgia in early 1919, they were not remembered as hated occupiers. And the esteem in which they were held by most Georgians would only go up after the experience with their successors, the British. In the collective memory of the Georgians, the Germans were esteemed.

The Experiment

During their three short years of independence, the Georgians had an opportunity to create an alternative to the regime Lenin and the Bolsheviks had established in Russia. Where Lenin had outlawed all other political parties, in Georgia a multi-party system was allowed to thrive. Where the Bolsheviks had dispersed the elected Constituent

Assembly at bayonet point, in Georgia free elections were held in which several parties competed and in which women could vote and run for office.

The Bolsheviks established an economy based on what they called 'war communism', which was in reality an undeclared war on the countryside. Detachments of armed workers would set out from the cities and seize food from the peasants. The result was mass starvation. In Georgia, the Social Democratic government took an entirely different approach. Land was given out to the peasants in a surprisingly efficient agrarian reform. The result was the beginning of a middle class in the countryside, one which was loyal to the Social Democrats and their republic. And there was no starvation in the cities.

Where the Bolsheviks had pushed for the militarisation of labour, in the process crushing the trade unions that had emerged in the revolution of 1917, in Georgia those unions were allowed to thrive. Though they demanded – and won – a constitutionally guaranteed right to strike, they hardly ever exercised that right. Instead, they worked with government and employers to set up, in May 1919, the Board of Wages, which regulated labour relations, kept wages in line with a rising cost of living, mediated between employers and employees when there was a dispute, and ensured that workers and their families had enough to eat. Their economic and social policies prefigured much of what occurred across Western Europe after the Second World War, with a 'social market economy' and powerful trade unions.

The Bolsheviks pushed – at least for a few years – to abolish the free market and capitalist property, resulting in the impoverishment of the entire society and a severe economic crisis. This eventually led to what Lenin called the 'new economic policy', a retreat back to the market economy which began in 1921 and only lasted for a few years. The Georgians embraced the mixed economy from the start, and gave special priority to the cooperative movement. The Georgian cooperatives thrived, and after a few short years had become the dominant factor in many sectors of the economy.

The Georgians did not create an ideal society. The country remained poor, and relations between the Georgians and ethnic minorities living within their borders were problematic. But it was never their intention to create a utopia. They aimed to create a better society, unlike the Bolsheviks who had utopian aims and applied ruthless measures to achieve them.

Stalin was one of the very few Georgians who loathed the local Social Democrats and preferred Lenin. Long isolated among the Georgian revolutionaries, Stalin spent most of his time in the years running up to 1917 either in St Petersburg or in Siberian exile. He was disliked and mistrusted in Georgia, suspected by many of being a police agent. As a Georgian, he was entrusted by Lenin with the task of formulating a Bolshevik policy on ethnic minorities and small nations, and wrote a short book on the subject. Once the Bolsheviks came to power in Russia, he took his place in their leadership. Lenin named him as the People's Commissar for Nationalities. He longed for a chance to take his revenge on the Georgians who had rejected him.

Georgia's experiment with democratic socialism stood in such stark contrast to what the Russian Bolsheviks were doing that it attracted the attention of Social Democrats across Europe. In September 1920 a delegation of leading figures in the British Labour Party as well as Social Democrats from France, Germany and Belgium came over to see what was actually happening in Georgia. The delegation included Karl Kautsky, the Belgians Emile Vandervelde and Camille Huysmans, as well as the British Labour leaders James Ramsay MacDonald (a future prime minister), Ethel Snowden and Tom Shaw. The French Socialist Party was represented by three leading politicians, Adrien Marquet among them.

We will return to Marquet later in this story, as his sympathy for the Georgians which was sparked by this visit was still strong two decades later during a very dark time.

All the Social Democratic delegates were very impressed with what they saw in Georgia. Kautsky went on to write a short book on the subject, as he stayed the longest in the country. Snowden, who had previously visited Soviet Russia and come away very critical of the Bolsheviks, said of the Georgians 'They have set up what is the most perfect Socialism in Europe.'

The Georgian experiment did not last. In February 1921, the Red Army invaded and over the course of a few weeks, defeated the Georgian Army and forced the Social Democratic government into exile. Many of the exiled leaders wound up in France, where they staked out their claim as Georgia's legitimate government.

Back home, the Georgians continued to resist Soviet rule, both with peaceful protest and, for a time, guerrilla warfare. The early attempts at armed resistance were futile, and as a result all the non-Bolshevik forces decided to unite and form a common front, aiming to drive the Soviets out. The result was a nationwide rebellion in August 1924 that led to thousands of deaths and gave a career boost to a local secret-police officer who would make a mark for himself in the USSR. His name was Lavrenty Beria and he would go on to become the most feared man in the Soviet Union as the head of Stalin's People's Commissariat for Internal Affairs (*Narodnyy Komissariat Vnutrennikh Del* – NKVD) . When Stalin introduced Beria to US President Franklin D. Roosevelt during the Yalta summit in 1945, he described him as 'our Himmler'.

The two decades between the Soviet invasion of Georgia in 1921 and the German invasion of the USSR – a time when the men at the centre of our story were growing up – were not a particularly happy time in Georgia, despite some industrialisation and modernisation.

Like the rest of the Soviet Union, the Georgian peasants were forced to part with their lands after their brief experience with the Social Democratic agrarian reform. Instead they were forced into *kolkhozes*, collective farms under the strict control of the Soviet state. And Georgia, like the rest of the Soviet Union, experienced the rise of the police state, the purges, the show trials, the labour camps, the knock on the door.

Chapter 2

Barbarossa

The most surprising thing about the German invasion of the Soviet Union on 22 June 1941 was that it was a surprise to anyone.

Operation Barbarossa had been in the works for many months, and by the eve of the invasion a vast quantity of soldiers, vehicles, aircraft and other equipment had been moved up to the border separating the Soviet Union from the German Reich. This was not a big secret, and Stalin had been receiving a steady stream of reports from his intelligence services confirming that a German invasion was about to happen.

More than three weeks before the Wehrmacht launched its attack, Soviet super-spy Richard Sorge sent on a report from Tokyo, where he had become a trusted adviser to a German diplomat. According to what Sorge had learned from his source, there was a 95 per cent chance that war between Nazi Germany and Soviet Russia was imminent. Stalin chose to ignore the message and characterised Sorge as a lying 'shit who has set himself up with some small factories and brothels in Japan'.[1] But it turned out that Sorge's intelligence was accurate.

Hitler had never concealed his hatred of the Soviet Union. He wrote about it in *Mein Kampf* and spoke about it quite openly. The Soviets had been keenly aware of the possibility of war with Nazi Germany, which is why they supported anti-fascist causes during most of the 1930s. It was obvious to all that the German fascists in power were going to represent a serious threat to the Soviet Union.

But after failing to reach an agreement with the Western powers to ensure the collective security of all the countries which were threatened by Nazi Germany, Stalin did a stunning turnaround and made a deal in August 1939 to prevent a German invasion of the Soviet Union. To the Germans, the Hitler–Stalin Pact meant that they would be essentially unopposed in their drive through Poland (except by the much-inferior Polish armed forces, which put up a determined though futile resistance). The Germans would also face no problem from their eastern neighbour when they turned their armies to the west in early 1940, conquering Denmark, Norway, the Netherlands, Belgium, Luxemburg and finally France.

They could count on the Soviets being neutral during the first twenty-two months of the world war, months in which the Germans would fight on one front and then another, with no fear of a debilitating 'war on two fronts', as had been the case in the First World War. And during the period of the Hitler–Stalin Pact, the Soviets provided Germany with considerable material assistance.

Once the war in the west was effectively over (with the notable exception of Britain, which remained stubbornly unoccupied), Hitler turned his attention again to the east. Only Stalin seemed unaware of this possibility.

Worse, Stalin had done all he could in the late 1930s to destroy the entire military leadership of the Soviet Union in his brutal purge of the Red Army. The vast majority of Soviet marshals and top generals were either executed, imprisoned or sent off to exile, accused by an increasingly paranoid dictator of plotting to seize power. Stalin's armies, once among the most powerful in Europe, had essentially been beheaded. Many of the men who would lead them in the early days of the Second World War were either inexperienced junior officers, or mediocrities who survived the purges by staying under the dictator's radar.

On the morning of 22 June 1941, the Germans launched the largest military operation ever. They hurled 148 divisions – around 3,200,000 soldiers – at the Soviet front lines, deploying some 3,350 tanks and 2,000 aircraft. Their army even used 600,000 horses – probably the last time in history that such a large equine force would be deployed in warfare. And Germany was not alone. Just as the Allied forces liked to imagine themselves as a 'United Nations' fighting for a just cause (the defeat of fascism), so the Germans had their own allied forces who joined their ranks in the battle against the Bolshevik 'menace'. These included soldiers from Romania, Italy, Finland, Hungary, Slovakia and Spain.

Never had an army moved so fast and taken so much territory. In the first few days of the fighting, four Panzer groups broke through the Soviet lines. Red Army troops had been pressed hard against the border because Soviet military doctrine specified that they were to carry the war to the territory of the enemy as quickly as possible. In reality, it took them nearly four years of hard fighting until they crossed the border into the Third Reich.

In the first week alone, the Germans advanced 400 km into the USSR. Once the German forces began their invasion across a broad front, it seemed that there was no stopping them. Within days, the capital of a Soviet republic, Belorussia's Minsk, was in German hands. It would be followed several weeks later by Kiev, the Ukrainian capital. The three Soviet Baltic republics – only recently occupied by the Red Army as part of the 1939 Hitler–Stalin Pact – quickly fell to the German forces, who were in many cases welcomed as liberators. One by one, the 'Soviet Socialist Republics' which comprised the USSR fell to the German advance.

Surrendering to the Germans

For the first few weeks, every Soviet army that stood in the Wehrmacht's path was either annihilated, forced to retreat, or encircled and compelled to surrender. Hundreds of thousands of Soviet soldiers quickly laid down their arms. The once-mighty Red Army seemed a spent force even before the war had really begun.

Following the early Soviet defeats in which large numbers of soldiers surrendered to the advancing German forces, Stalin issued the infamous Order No. 270 in August 1941. Red Army personnel were instructed to fight to the last; he banned officers from surrendering and imposed severe punishments on deserters. Men were ordered to save their last bullet for themselves.

The order went far beyond what would normally be seen in other armies, though most countries had harsh penalties for desertion, often including execution. The British Army, for example, executed over 300 deserters during the First World War. What distinguished Stalin's order and made it particularly monstrous was that family members of those who surrendered to the Germans or deserted were subject to arrest. Family members could also be deprived of any form of state support.

'There are no Soviet prisoners of war,' Stalin said, 'only *traitors*.'

But there *were* Soviet prisoners of war, millions of them. According to some estimates, a total of over five million surrendered to the Germans. What motivated men to surrender was usually the fear of the alternative, which was certain death. But the tragic irony for Soviet soldiers was that there was ultimately little difference between dying on the battlefield and the fate that awaited them in German camps.

Millions of them died in German captivity, where they starved, or froze to death, or fell victim to epidemics, or were shot. By May 1944, of the five million Soviet soldiers who had fallen into German hands, some two million were recorded as having died in prisoner of war camps. Another 1.3 million were designated as exterminated or not accounted for, with a very small fraction of those being prisoners who had escaped.[2]

Some of them were killed intentionally and immediately. The Germans had specific orders to shoot any captured Soviet political commissars, who were the representatives of the Communist Party inside the army. And even before the Holocaust had begun in earnest, the Nazis were killing every single Jewish Red Army soldier who fell into their hands.

The wholesale mass murder of Soviet prisoners was not planned and was the result of a number of factors. These included a lack of German preparedness, the failure of the Soviets to be signatories to the Geneva Convention (thus depriving their prisoners of any legal protection) and in general, German brutality toward those it classed as *Untermenschen* (sub-humans).

The application of the Germans' racist views to the captured prisoners led to some incredible blunders. For example, because Jewish soldiers were to be executed immediately, the Germans needed a way to identify them quickly. One way was to check captured Soviet soldiers to see if they had been circumcised. But as it turned out, not all circumcised men were Jews. Muslim soldiers, for example, tended to also be circumcised. As a result, for many months, thousands of Muslims and even individuals who 'looked Jewish' were murdered on their capture. Later on, the Germans would make a determined effort to recruit Muslims into their ranks and to win support in Islamic countries. Shooting captured Muslim Red Army soldiers was not a good beginning to that effort.

The Germans separated the captured Russians from the other Soviet nationalities, such as the Belorussians and Ukrainians. The German attitude toward the non-Russian prisoners was influenced by the opinions of academic Orientalists and friendly diplomats (including Turkish ones), and as a result prisoners of war who were Crimean Tatars, Balkars, Karachais, Chechens and Circassians were often treated as Aryans.

Among those who were kept separate were the Georgians, who have been described as 'the favourites of the Ostministerium' – the ministry for the occupied territories, headed by Alfred Rosenberg. This would have been due to the history of positive Georgian–German relations going back to the First World War, as well as the existence of a community of exiled Georgians living in Germany who were sympathetic to the Nazis. We'll meet them later in this story.

There was a brief moment when the leaders of the German Army understood that it was in their best interest to release a fairly large number of prisoners – on the condition that they belonged to Soviet nations that were believed to be more sympathetic to Germany than the Russians, and whose territory was now occupied by the Wehrmacht. Large numbers of Ukrainian and Belorussian POWs were released to their families, and in some cases to civilians *pretending* to be their families, and they were all told that Hitler had done them a huge favour. This of course would not have been the case for Georgian prisoners, as the German Army at no point occupied their country. They were not released.

The German occupation authorities in Ukraine and Belorussia then panicked, believing that many of these men would quickly join the new partisan forces fighting against the Germans, behind the front lines. For many of the released prisoners, this turned out to be the case, and the brief experiment in leniency toward captured Soviet troops largely ended.

Meanwhile, the prisoners remaining in German hands were suffering a terrible fate. 'While Berlin argued and the armies fought,' wrote Alexander Dallin, the historian of the German occupation of Russia,

> the prisoners died. Testimony is eloquent and prolific on the abandonment of entire divisions under the open sky. Epidemics and endemic diseases decimated the camps. Beatings and abuse by the guards were commonplace. Millions spent weeks without food or shelter. Carloads of prisoners were dead before they arrived at their destination. Casualty figures varied considerably but almost nowhere amounted to less than 30 per cent in the winter of 1941–2, and sometimes went as high as 95 per cent.[3]

The Germans made much of reported cases of cannibalism among the prisoners. Hermann Göring told Galeazzo Ciano, Mussolini's foreign minister (and son-in-law), that in the prisoner of war camps, 'After having eaten everything possible, including the soles of their boots, they have begun to eat each other, and what is more serious, have also eaten a German sentry.'[4] Hitler was quoted as saying to a Danish minister, 'Do you know that these are all *Untermenschen?* Cannibals! They eat each other up.'[5] The Nazis used these stories to illustrate their conviction that the Soviet prisoners were less than human. As we shall see, when the Georgians arrived on Texel some years later, Dutch civilians there were warned that these men might well be cannibals.

In treating Soviet prisoners this way, the Germans were acting against their own interests. Many of those prisoners could have been working in Germany, as the Third Reich suffered a persistent shortage of labourers. Russian civilians were imported in large numbers to fill the gap – as were prisoners of war. At one point, realising that the Soviet prisoners were so weak from starvation that they could not work as slave labourers, one of Himmler's friends suggested that if half the prisoners could be shot, the Germans could double the rations for the survivors and make them more useful for the Reich. His suggestion was not adopted.

The prisoners were dying in such vast quantities, especially in the first winter of the war, that at one point the head of the Gestapo protested, saying that commandants of concentration camps under his command were complaining that five to ten percent of the Soviet captives who had been sent to them to be shot were already dead by the time they arrived in the camps.

The mistreatment of the Soviet prisoners of war became known in the USSR, in part due to Soviet propaganda, and this made the Red Army an even more determined opponent. Soldiers were less likely to surrender or desert if the result was the same or worse than dying in battle. The German mistreatment of Red Army prisoners also became known to the vast numbers of Soviet citizens now living under German occupation. They were genuinely shocked at the stories of the horrific treatment of the prisoners. This undermined any sympathy they may have felt for the occupiers. The number of deserters from Soviet ranks began to drop month on month thanks to the German decision to mistreat all captured Soviet soldiers, including those who had voluntarily crossed over to the German lines. And later on it made the recruitment of Soviet prisoners into the 'Eastern Battalions' which the Germans would eventually form – the Georgian Legion among them – far more difficult.

The mass deaths of Soviet prisoners were largely a feature of the first winter of the war on the Eastern Front, and afterwards conditions improved slightly. The improvement took place not because the Germans suddenly became humanitarians, but because as the war dragged on, the need for Soviet prisoners to become slave labourers in Germany became more acute. The Germans now had a reason to keep their Soviet prisoners alive.

Despite the relative improvement of conditions for the prisoners following the winter of 1941–2, the damage had been done, and the Germans had missed an opportunity to turn at least some Red Army soldiers into willing allies of the Reich.

Although the survival rate of Soviet prisoners held by the Germans was appalling, the survival rate of German prisoners in Soviet hands was a bit worse, and what's more the average prisoner who survived lived for longer in German captivity.

The German Advance on Georgia

The South Caucasus was a major target for the German forces as they advanced across the Soviet Union in the summer of 1941. This was the case in the Second World War for the same reason as it was in the First: the oil of Azerbaijan and the mineral deposits of Georgia were vital strategic assets.

As in other parts of the Soviet Union, one of the first groups to suffer during the war was the ethnic German population. Karl Kautsky had written favourably about the German agricultural colonists in Georgia in his book two decades earlier. But by 1941, over 19,000 ethnic Germans living in Georgia were seen as a potential threat by the Communist government, and were deported to Kazakhstan.

Meanwhile, about 100,000 Georgians serving in the Red Army were sent to the front, many of them to be killed or captured by the Germans. Overall during the course of the war, some 550,000 Georgians served with the Soviet forces, and the majority of them did not return. Many of them died in the battles in Crimea and the Kerch peninsula. The total losses for Georgia during the war, including higher infant mortality, may have reached 700,000, or one-fifth of the country's population. It was a demographic catastrophe whose effects can be felt right up to the present day.[6]

It is vitally important to remember those numbers as we discuss those Georgians who wound up wearing German uniforms. They were a minority, a small minority, compared to the enormous number of Georgians who fought and died in the battles against the Nazi Germans.

As German troops raced through southern Russia on their way to the Caucasus, Stalin sent Beria, a fellow Georgian and head of his secret police, to Tbilisi to strengthen local resistance to the Nazi onslaught. Elite forces of the NKVD were attached to the Red Army, and Georgians believed to be nationalistic or sympathetic to the Germans were purged.

German forces never made it much beyond the Georgian frontier in their drive to the Caucasus, having been diverted at Stalingrad. The Germans managed to drop a few bombs on the Georgian cities of Sukhumi, Poti, and Tbilisi, and it did look for a time as if they might cross into Georgia. German alpine troops climbed Mount Elbrus, the highest peak in the Caucasus, just north of Georgia, where they planted a swastika flag on the summit. They held the area for about six months, and managed to enter some of the high passes in the Caucasus range. For a few days, some German troops held a small area of the country. One group managed briefly to occupy an Abkhaz village. But on the whole, the Soviet forces – with the help of snow – held the Germans back. Georgia was never occupied.

Ironically, as the German forces began their retreat, they were joined by thousands of Soviet Georgian troops, who were seduced by radio broadcasts, loudspeaker messages and leaflets in their language. Meanwhile, behind the German lines, the Georgians who had switched sides found some well-known Georgian generals awaiting them. After a while, some Germans 'complained that they were feeding and training more Georgians than they were fighting'.[7]

Eventually, some Georgians would be allowed to take up arms on the German side in the war – much more on this later – but it's very important to understand the broader picture. And a picture to keep in mind is the famous photo of two Red Army soldiers raising the Soviet flag over the ruins of the Reichstag in Berlin on May Day in 1945.

One of those men was Sergeant Mikhail A. Yegorov, a Russian. The other was Sergeant Meliton Kantaria, a Georgian. Kantaria was chosen because the Soviet leadership wanted to symbolise the fact that the Red Army represented many different nationalities, and not only Russians. Why specifically a Georgian was chosen, presumably with Stalin's approval, is an interesting question. Perhaps Stalin wanted to emphasise that, though he was the leader of the entire Soviet Union, he was also a Georgian. Or perhaps it was a way to counter the influence of the Georgian émigrés, many of whom were Social Democrats.

In any event, that photograph of Kantaria standing atop the ruins of the Third Reich is a stark reminder that Georgians, like all the other Soviet peoples, contributed much to the victory over Nazi Germany.

Chapter 3

The Exiles

During the 1920s and 1930s, a number of Georgians found themselves living in exile in western and central Europe. With the outbreak of the Second World War in 1939, and particularly following the German invasion of the Soviet Union two years later, they broke up roughly into two camps.

On the one side were those, led by the Social Democratic government-in-exile, who were anti-Nazi and did what they could to survive during a terrible period. On the other side were those who saw in the Third Reich an ally in the fight to restore Georgian independence. What both sides agreed upon was that the war would almost certainly lead to the downfall of the Stalin regime – and on that point, as we now know, both sides were proved wrong.

The Rescue of the Georgian Jews

Georgia was one of the few countries in the world to lack a history of anti-semitism. This was not the case elsewhere in the Soviet Union, and there were many examples of local Soviet populations welcoming the Germans not only as liberators, but also collaborating with them in the Holocaust. To this day, this remains a matter of controversy in several of the post-Soviet republics.

In Georgia, a thriving Jewish community had been part of the country for centuries. With the collapse of the tsarist regime in 1917, the Jews of Georgia – like Jews throughout the former Russian Empire – were liberated. Some went on to play important roles in Georgia's Social Democratic government.

During the three years in which Georgia was independent, the local Zionist movement took off, creating Jewish educational and cultural institutions in the country. They founded a Jewish school in Tbilisi and a bi-weekly newspaper with a wide circulation. The Georgian Jews at that time were divided between Zionist and non-Zionist wings, with the latter faring better in the new democratic order. Three seats in the Constituent Assembly were reserved for Jews, two of whom became signers of the Declaration of Independence. One of them was Iosif Eligoulashvili, a Jewish Social Democrat who served as Deputy Minister of Finance, Trade and Industry. Following the Soviet invasion of Georgia in 1921, Eligoulashvili joined the other Social Democratic leaders in exile in France. His was one of about forty Georgian Jewish families in Paris which quickly formed ties with the French Jewish community.

While the majority of the Georgians in exile supported the Social Democrats, there were some who backed the more right-wing parties, including the National Democrats and the Socialist Federalists – more on these in a moment. Among the Georgians living in France, there were few signs of anti-semitism, and there were even Jews among the leaders of the right-wing Georgian parties.

Those three parties were forced to work closely together after June 1941 as they became increasingly convinced that a German victory in the war with the Soviet Union was inevitable, and that Georgian independence would once more be on the agenda. The Social Democrats had an expectation not shared by the others that in the long run the Allies would prevail over Germany – but in the meantime, Georgia would be set free from Soviet rule.

Meanwhile, one segment of the Georgian exile community in France faced a particular threat. In July 1940, following the German victory over the French and the occupation of most of the country, Adrien Marquet, the Minister of the Interior in the Vichy government, warned the Georgian leaders that an order was about to be issued requiring all Jews in France to register with the police. Marquet was a former leader of the French Socialist Party, and one of the participants in the 1920 international socialist delegation to Georgia. He knew the Georgian Social Democratic leaders personally. Though he served in the Vichy government, he did not see himself as an anti-semite and later resigned his post to protest anti-Jewish measures. In 1940, he told the Georgian exiles, 'I don't want to give a hand to this dirty thing,' referring to the new anti-Jewish laws.

The Georgians, Eligoulashvili among them, always insisted that Marquet was being honest. He was not paid for the help he gave to the Georgian Jews. And his later resignation from the Vichy government proved that, they said. After the war, his actions regarding the Georgian Jews helped him when he stood trial for his role in Vichy.

As Marquet had predicted, the order for all Jews to report to the police was issued, but the Georgian leadership had a clear message for the Jewish community: 'We forbid you to register.' The Georgian president in exile, Noe Zhordania, and Evgeni Gegechkori, the foreign minister, met with ten Georgian Jewish leaders to pass on that instruction.

The Jewish community trusted the Social Democratic leaders and did not register with the police. Eligoulashvili's nephew, Levi, who later told the story of the rescue of the Georgian Jews in France, was then in Paris and expressed concern that there was no legal basis for the refusal to register with the police. He thought this dangerous. The Georgian leaders assured him that an official exemption would be obtained somehow from the Germans. And an exemption was indeed obtained – possibly because the German authorities wanted to keep up a good relationship with the Georgian exile community at that time.

The Georgian Jews in France did not register with the police, nor were they compelled to obey the anti-Jewish laws that were coming into force. They were helped in this by the fact that they tended to have Georgian-sounding names, and that they appeared to be no different from other Georgians.

Still, the decision to exempt the Georgian Jews was based on instructions sent by Berlin to the German military authorities in Paris, and this was a matter of some concern to the Jewish community. The Vichy minister Marquet was again approached and asked to sort this all out officially between the Vichy regime and the German occupation authorities.

Marquet did as he promised, and the Georgian Jews were formally exempted from the anti-Jewish laws. The French police were instructed to treat them as non-Jews. The Jewish community then asked for the non-Jewish Georgian leadership to appoint a committee to decide who received the special status of being a Georgian Jew. Those given that status would be issued with special identity cards which would prove their exemption from the anti-Jewish laws. The committee was established and it began making its lists.

Incredibly, the list eventually contained some 243 families with about 1,000 individuals. At the time, there were only about forty Jewish families among the Georgians in France. Clearly the vast majority of those on the lists were Jews who did not come from Georgia. The Georgian leadership had decided to use this loophole to rescue hundreds of non-Georgian Jews. Many of those were given Georgian names to help cover the fact that they were not Georgian at all.

The identity cards which were issued to these people saved their lives. There were cases where people were arrested and quickly released thanks to the cards. This worked well for a time – until the Germans started losing the war on the Eastern Front. Once it became clear that German troops were never going to make it to Georgia, the Nazis lost all interest in the Georgian exiles, and in particular in the concessions they previously made to them.

By 1943, the situation had got far worse. One Georgian Jewish family was caught in a house in Lyon, where Vichy militia did a search. They found Jewish prayer shawls and *tefillin* (the small leather boxes containing readings from the Hebrew Bible worn by religious Jews when they pray). The family members were arrested and taken to the detention camp at Drancy, a northern suburb of Paris. It was from Drancy that tens of thousands of French Jews began their journeys to the death camps of Auschwitz and elsewhere. Fortunately, after two or three weeks of negotiations, the Georgian exile leaders managed to get them released – though one of the Georgian leaders had to travel to Berlin to arrange this. For the Georgian Jews, this was a worrying sign.

A year later, shortly before the liberation of France by Allied forces, Iosif Eligoulashvili's brother-in-law was arrested in Nice and taken to Drancy. He was not so lucky, and the efforts of the Georgian exile leaders were not successful this time. He was transported to the east and never heard from again. At this point, the Georgian Jews in France all went into hiding. Fortunately, they remained hidden until the end of the war.[1]

Meanwhile, the German Army had failed in its efforts to reach Georgia, thus saving the lives of members of the country's long-established Jewish community there. But in their approach to the Georgian border in 1942, an opportunity was created for at least one Georgian to step forward and save Jewish lives. For his efforts, Sergey Metreveli, a Georgian from the village of Utsera, was recognised on 24 June 2004 by Yad Vashem, the World Holocaust Remembrance Center in Jerusalem, as a 'Righteous Among the Nations'. This is what Yad Vashem has to say about what he did to earn it:

> Sergey Metreveli and Ivan Gugeshashvili were wine producers in Kislovodsk, a town in the northern Caucasus. At the end of August 1942, as the German forces were approaching the town, the two men evacuated Jews and other people known as Communists, in order to save them from the Germans. Emil Zigel and Arkadi Rabinovich were among the endangered Jews. In August 1941, when Emil was 16 he had gone with his parents, from Dnepropetrovsk in the Ukraine to Kislovodsk. Emil was the youngest of the five Zigel children. His elder brothers Moisei, Naum, and Samuil had been conscripted into the Red Army when Germany invaded the USSR and all three died in combat during 1941–1942. The only sister, Vera, was studying medicine in Voroshilovsk (currently Stavropol). For 16 days during the autumn of 1942 the sad line of fleeing refugees, led by Sergey Metreveli, moved through the Caucasian mountains. After marching some 500 km, they came to Sergey's home village of Utsera (Oni County) on the Georgian side of the Caucasian range that had not been conquered by the Germans. Sergey's parents and family lived there. Arakdi Rabinovich and other members of the group continued on their way to the main Georgian cities, but Emil, who had contracted malaria, was forced to stay behind in the village. The Metreveli family cared for him over several weeks, until he recovered. Thus, with their help, and especially that of Sergey Metreveli, Emil survived

the fate of his parents who had remained in Kislovodosk. In September 1942, the Germans removed all the Jews of the city, among them Ekaterina and Enoch (Heinrich) Zigel, to the nearby town of Mineralnye Vody and murdered them there. In mid-September 1942, Emil came to the Ural region and several months later enlisted in the Red Army. He became an officer and in 1946 visited his rescuers in their village and continued to keep in contact with them.[2]

Of the nearly 27,000 people recognised for their work rescuing Jews, Metreveli is the only Georgian to have been accorded that honour.

The Pro-Nazi Georgians in Exile

While many of the Georgians in exile were hoping for an Allied victory in the war, others were more sympathetic to the Nazis. These individuals were later instrumental in recruiting Georgian soldiers who had been captured by the Germans into a new 'Georgian Legion' which would fight on the German side in the war.

One of them was General Leo Kereselidze, who had participated in the Russian Revolution of 1905, and after its defeat moved to Western Europe where he became active in Georgian separatist groups. During the First World War, these groups had a pro-German orientation and were based in Berlin. Kereselidze was instrumental in the formation of the Georgian Legion that took Germany's side in that war, and he was promoted to the rank of major-general. After the dissolution of the Georgian Legion in 1917, he returned to Georgia where he played a role in the new Georgian Army during the period of independence. After the Soviet invasion in 1921 he found himself again in exile in Germany where he was among the founders of the fascist 'White George' organisation.

Another was Prince Mikheil Tsereteli. Tsereteli studied in Germany before the outbreak of the First World War and during the war worked as an assistant professor at Berlin University. He also headed the Committee of Independent Georgia, a nationalist organisation. Once Georgia achieved its independence in 1918, he served as its ambassador to Sweden and Norway, later returning to the country to teach at Tbilisi

State University, which was founded in 1918. Following the Soviet invasion in 1921, Tsereteli once again left the country, first teaching in Brussels and later in Berlin. He also headed up the 'Georgian National Committee', which had bases in Berlin and Paris, and he too was linked to the Georgian fascist organisation 'White George'.[3]

And yet another key figure in the pro-German wing of the Georgian exile community was Alexander Nikuradze. Like Tsereteli, he studied in Berlin and stayed there after the crushing of the independent Georgian state in 1921. He became a German citizen and was closely tied to the Nazis. He befriended Alfred Rosenberg in the 1920s when both were exiles living in Munich, and he helped shape Rosenberg's views about the Caucasus region. This became important once Rosenberg, an ardent Nazi, took charge of the Ostministerium, the Nazi government ministry responsible for the occupied eastern territories. Nikuradze advocated a German protectorate over a future Caucasian federation which would be dominated by Georgia – not unlike the situation in the Caucasus back in 1918.

From the moment the German Army crossed the Soviet frontier in June 1941, Kereselidze, Tsereteli and Nikuradze were among those who provided the ideological justification for Georgians supporting the Third Reich in the war against the Soviet Union. To help fund their efforts, the Germans gave them control over four factories that had belonged to Jewish owners in Warsaw. A committee was established to coordinate their efforts and it included General Shalva Maglakelidze, whom we will meet later on, and Seid Shamil. Shamil was the grandson of the imam Shamil, a legendary warrior who had led a determined resistance to the expansion of Russian rule in the Caucasus in the nineteenth century.

These Georgian émigrés had a vision for the future. They imagined that, following the defeat of the Soviet armies, the Germans would turn Georgia into a protectorate, as they had done with Slovakia. Or perhaps they were inspired by the model of the benign German occupation of Georgia in 1918. The Germans encouraged these émigré Georgians to propose General Maglakelidze as a Georgian *Führer*.

The Georgian diaspora seemed well suited to be allies of the Germans, with its proliferation of traditionally pro-German leaders and with its memories of the 1918 German occupation of Georgia still fresh. But things were not so simple. The NKVD infiltrated the Georgians who switched over to the German side, doing their own recruiting in the POW camps. There were attempts made to assassinate the turncoat leaders in Germany; two agents were sent on an unsuccessful mission to liquidate General Maglakelidze. There was even an attempt to lure him back to Georgia to take charge of a non-existent rebellion there.

German efforts to infiltrate their own men, including Georgians now serving on their side, into Georgia were generally failures. At one point the Germans sent seven men into Georgia, dropped from a plane, but four of them turned out to be NKVD agents. The 30 men and 30 million roubles which followed them were wasted.

There were further attempts by the Germans to parachute Georgians into the country to work on behalf of the Reich. But every single one of the parachutists was captured or surrendered within a few days. Near the Georgian city of Kutaisi, eight of the Georgian parachutists turned themselves in – but they were forcibly taken back to where they had landed and publicly shot there.

But while these sporadic efforts to use Georgians to undermine Soviet rule in the Caucasus failed to achieve their goals, the Germans were developing a far more ambitious project: the Bergmann Battalion.

Chapter 4

Sonderverband *Bergmann*

In the two years between the German invasion of the Soviet Union in June 1941 and the formation of the Georgian Legion in June 1943, there were few opportunities for Georgian prisoners of war or émigrés to play a role in the war against the Stalin regime. This was due in large part to German resistance to the idea of arming former Soviet soldiers, and Hitler's strong belief that these were mostly *Untermenschen* who should never be trusted.

But on the margins of the Nazi war machine, in the Abwehr, the military intelligence service of the Armed Forces High Command, a plan was hatched to allow some former Soviet soldiers and some men from the émigré communities to play a part in the war. In October 1941, some 400 former Soviet soldiers, all of them from the Caucasus region, were removed from the POW camps in which they were starving to death. They were farmed out to local villages to recover their strength. A few weeks later, they were taken to the Strans training camp outside Neuhammer, a town in Silesia. There Sonderverband *Bergmann* was formed as part of the larger Brandenburg Regiment.

The Brandenburgers were an élite formation. They played pivotal roles in the invasion of the Soviet Union and other countries, going in before the regular army and carrying out acts of sabotage. They were highly trained soldiers, often fluent in foreign languages, who could operate far behind the front lines. A highly decorated unit, the Brandenburgers continued playing their special role until September 1944 when they were incorporated back into the regular army.

The initial group of prisoners were joined at the Strans camp over the next few months by other groups of former prisoners, including one group of 'Mensheviks' under the command of Lieutenant Shaliko (Shalva) Okropiridze.

It was not only former Soviet POWs who volunteered to serve in the newly formed Bergmann Battalion. About 130 Georgian émigrés also came forward to join it as well. Many of these men had previously served in the French Army – France being the country where many Georgian exiles lived, and where their government-in-exile had been based. Those men, commanded by Lieutenant Tsiklauri and later by Lieutenant Gabliani, were put into a special unit called 'Tamar - 2'. This special force was created as an élite, pro-Nazi formation, but later suffered from desertions, and was eventually seen as unreliable by the Germans.

The formation of the Bergmann Battalion, which had an initial strength of 800 men, gave Georgians and other Caucasians their first opportunity to take up arms against the Soviet Union.[1]

The Germans liked to think that the Georgians and others who joined the ranks of the battalion did so for ideological reasons, hoping that a German victory in the war would lead to the liberation of their homeland from Soviet rule. But there can be little doubt that hunger may have been more of a factor. While Soviet POWs were starving to death in German camps, the Bergmann volunteers received several meals per day, including hot food. According to one source, this was at least 450–600 grams of bread, 25 grams of sausage, 30 grams of butter or margarine, sweet tea or coffee and several cigarettes.[2]

Eventually, the battalion would consist of five companies of volunteers. One of those companies was made up entirely of Georgians and Armenians, one was nearly all Georgians, and the others included Azerbaijanis and North Caucasians. The unit grew over time, and by the spring of 1943, it had expanded into a regiment with three battalions.

At the same time as the Bergmann Battalion was growing into a regiment, Stalin began creating national divisions in the Red Army. Several Georgian divisions were deployed to defend the Caucasus. It is said that Georgian officers would swear at each other in their native tongue from the opposing trenches.

All the officers in the Bergmann Battalion were Germans, and this practice would continue throughout the war. Even in the Georgian

Legion, formed some time later, the officers were almost entirely Germans. In the Bergmann Battalion, foremost among those officers was Oberleutnant Theodor Oberländer, formerly an economics professor at the University of Königsberg and a Nazi.

Before the war, Oberländer had researched the reasons for the defeat of the anti-Bolshevik White armies in the Russian civil war of 1918–21. In his view, the main reason for the defeat of the Whites was 'insufficient attention' being paid to 'the national aspirations of the peoples of Russia and the unsettled issue of land ownership'.[3] In the current war, Oberländer was keen for Germany not to repeat these mistakes.

He became an enthusiastic proponent of the idea that national minorities in the Soviet Union, and primarily the Ukrainians, should be mobilised by the Germans to fight against Bolshevik Russia. Oberländer advocated the formation of 'liberation legions' for all the various national groups. As someone fluent in Georgian who could also communicate in other Caucasian languages, he wanted to test out his ideas on the Georgians and their neighbours in the Caucasus. But his plan had little support among the Nazi leadership at a time when the German armies seemed to be doing quite well on their own in their fight against the Red Army, as was the case throughout 1941.

When he could not get this idea adopted by the Army, he found another way: through the Abwehr, which had a certain amount of leeway that the Army High Command lacked. Oberländer was named as commander of the newly formed Bergmann unit.

As Alexander Dallin wrote, 'The relatively easy acceptance of this unit in Nazi circles was due largely to the fact that it was an intelligence-promoted enterprise and that "it was without the obvious political background or purpose."'[4]

There was a strong Georgian presence in the Bergmann Battalion from the start. The first men to join the ranks of the Bergmann Battalion were volunteers from the émigré community. But there were also Soviet Georgian prisoners of war who were recruited directly from POW camps in Romania. (One of the leaders of the Georgian uprising on Texel, Evgeni Artemidze, told his family that he was recruited from a POW camp in Romania – but it is not clear if this was to the Georgian

Legion, which was formed later on, or to the Bergmann group.)

Oberländer himself and his aides personally visited POW camps to find suitable candidates to join the battalion. At first, there were many more volunteers than were needed for the small unit. Later in the war, the Germans would struggle to recruit foreigners to serve in their armed forces, especially when their defeat seemed certain, but this was not the case in 1941. Oberländer was helped by Baron Walter von Kutsenbach, who was born in Tbilisi and could speak Georgian and other local languages.

Training took place at Neuhammer and Mittenwald. Five months after its formation, the battalion had over 1,000 men. But it was not until August 1942, some ten months after its formation, that the Bergmann troops were finally deployed to the Eastern Front.

They went into action in the North Caucasus campaign. Their primary role was the fight against Soviet partisans, as well as conducting reconnaissance and engaging in sabotage operations around Grozny. Towards the end of the year, the battalion conducted a successful raid through the Red Army lines, bringing back some 300 defectors.

The conduct of the Bergmann troops came under public scrutiny many years after the war. In 1959, the East Germans launched a public campaign to embarrass the West German Adenauer government which had named Theodor Oberländer as its federal minister for refugees some six years earlier. The 'Committee for German Unity', based in East Berlin, published a 'Brown Book' documenting Oberländer's war record. Though one should take the evidence presented by the East German Communists with a grain of salt, the fact is that Oberländer was forced to resign following the revelations. The 'Brown Book' is a rare find, but the London Library has a copy. A significant part of the tale it tells is the story of the Bergmann Battalion, which Oberländer headed.[5]

According to eyewitness testimony, mostly from Soviet citizens, Oberländer's claim that he did not actually command these troops was shown to be completely false. And he was depicted as a particularly brutal commander. According to one account, when some of the former Soviet POWs who were being trained to be part of the battalion formed an underground cell, Oberländer ordered their execution. Seven prisoners were shot. (Though some would say that this was not particularly cruel and was a common practice in many armies.)

Oberländer was considered a ruthless officer, cruel even to his own loyal troops. One former Soviet POW who signed up to join the battalion described Oberländer in this way: 'He was of average height, slim, round face, dark-blond hair. I remember him as a very heartless man.' He remembered one incident in particular. 'I witnessed the harsh way in which he treated a soldier of the battalion who was sick and could not do duty one day. [Oberländer] grabbed the sick soldier by his collar and threw him out on the ice-cold street. Such things happened very often.'[6]

The Bergmann Battalion, according to one witness,

> did not participate in any active fighting against the Soviet troops, but was employed as [a] punitive battalion in order to find out and liquidate Soviet patriots who had joined the partisans and were operating in the mountains behind the back of the German Nazis. The battalion was also employed against citizens who supported the partisans.[7]

One veteran of the battalion remembered,

> When we arrived in the Caucasus it became our task to liquidate the partisans who were operating in the near hinterland of the fascists, as well as those citizens who sympathised with the partisans and who supported them or had any contact with them.

He added that the entire battalion was occupied with anti-partisan warfare from October 1942 onwards, and insisted that Oberländer personally commanded the troops. 'This I know for sure,' he added, 'because at that time I was not anymore [a] private, but [a] group leader ... I can swear to this because I received orders myself from my company commander, which had been signed by Oberländer personally.' The punitive expeditions carried out by the Bergmann force 'cost hundreds of lives', according to the East German report. 'Innumerable Soviet citizens and soldiers were badly tortured and killed by Oberländer's command.'[8]

Oberländer himself was accused of setting an example 'for the brutal actions of this special unit to his subordinates by his reckless behaviour and by mistreating Soviet citizens'.[9] 'I learned more than once from my comrades how badly he treated the people,' remembered Asis Zuganov,

> I have not seen it myself, but I heard from many that he beat up Soviet citizens himself. He also ordered his men to do the same thing. Then he had the Soviet citizens brought to a special unit of his staff, where they were interrogated. I do not know what happened to those citizens, but none of us ever saw them again.[10]

Despite Oberländer's reputation for brutality, the Bergmann Battalion achieved some notable successes at first. As a result of its activity, including effective propaganda, the Soviet forces in the Caucasus suffered very high levels of desertions to the German side. For example, around 2,000 men deserted from the 392nd Rifle Division, a Soviet Georgian unit, in September 1942, and another two battalions also switched sides. Not all the Georgians who wanted to cross over to the German side succeeded in doing so. In the 394th Rifle Division, some eighty Georgians who attempted to desert were caught and shot by the NKVD in August 1942.

Things got so bad for the Red Army, which was losing large numbers of Caucasian recruits to the German side, that a decision was taken to transfer them to another part of the front. And thanks to the efforts of the Bergmann unit, the Germans were provoking unrest and uprisings behind the Soviet lines, exploiting national resentment against the Russians. The well-trained Bergmann troops also proved effective in their role as saboteurs, famously blowing up a bridge which delayed a Soviet retreat and also blowing up a Red Army train filled with equipment. As one historian put it, the Bergmann troops 'persistently proved their courage, motivation and belief in an ultimate German victory'.[11]

Eduard Abramian wrote:

> All the members of the Bergmann battalion, whether they fought on the front-lines or in the rear against Soviet partisans, always showed a disregard for their own lives. There were cases when

after a particularly bloody battle the unit had lost about 40% of its effective strength. Yet the soldiers went on fighting, setting an example for the other soldiers serving with the Wehrmacht.[12]

In one battle along the Sivash River, soldiers of the Georgian 1st Battalion of the Bergmann Regiment managed to stop a Red Army advance, but at the cost of 170 men. Their accomplishments and sacrifices were such that the First Panzer Army allowed the battalion to recruit another four companies of volunteers beginning in September 1942.

While some of the fighting done by the Bergmann force led to displays of bravery, others were characterised by savagery. Soviet partisans were quite active in the Caucasus, and partisan snipers were particularly effective in their attacks on the Bergmann volunteers. According to one report, the frustrated Bergmann soldiers,

> took part in a punitive action against the Soviet partisans in the region of Mineralnye Vody. It was there that the Bergmann soldiers took revenge for comrades who had been killed by guerrilla units, by taking forty villagers from their houses and shooting them as 'partisan suspects'.[13]

The drive into the Caucasus halted too soon from the German point of view, leaving Georgia unconquered and – more important – the oil fields of Baku out of reach. The Bergmann Battalion's soldiers never did get the opportunity to throw the Bolsheviks out from their Georgian homeland. Instead, they assisted the Germans with an orderly retreat from the region.

They were then deployed in the Crimea in early 1943 where they again participated in anti-partisan actions as well as engaging regular Soviet forces. But they increasingly lost their edge as an élite fighting force, no longer able to go behind Soviet lines and carry out the sabotage that had earlier made their reputation. Some of them now spent their time guarding railway lines and Crimea's long coastline.

A Soviet intelligence report at the time claimed that the various Caucasian forces now serving with the Germans in the Crimea were becoming increasingly unreliable. 'The political and moral state of the units ... is unstable ... This is especially conspicuous among the Georgians. Most of the Georgians, comprising about 60% of the division, are expecting that Soviet strength will prevail.'[14]

In October–November 1943, there were reports of 134 Georgians switching sides and signing up to join a Soviet partisan brigade. A special partisan detachment of eighty-five Georgians, who had formerly served the Germans, was now under the command of one Ilyasov. They fought against the Germans with weapons the Germans had provided to them.

As the war dragged on, and manpower shortages in their army became acute, the Nazi leadership grew increasingly aware of the necessity of creating the 'liberation legions' that Theodor Oberländer had advocated as early as 1941. The Bergmann Battalion was broken up into its various national components and these were moved further away from the Eastern Front where there were fears that former Soviet soldiers would prove to be unreliable allies for the German Army. Some were deployed to Poland and others to Greece.

Once in Greece many of the previously enthusiastic Bergmann soldiers seemed to have lost the will to fight. 'The volunteers did not understand how they were fighting to free their beloved Georgia from Stalin and communism by struggling against Greek freedom fighters.'[15] Eventually, some forty Georgian soldiers deserted to the Greek partisans, who were members of the Communist-led Greek People's Liberation Army (ELAS) forces.

Eventually, all the Eastern Battalions were deployed to the West, far from the influence of Soviet propaganda.

In 1944, veterans of the Bergmann Battalion were involved together with the SS in the brutal suppression of the Warsaw Rising, though by this time the Georgians were not among them. They were now integrated into the newly formed Georgian Legion.

Some of them may even have wound up with the 822nd Battalion, who were posted to Texel in 1945.

Chapter 5

Recruiting the Georgians

'All Enemies of the Reich – Step Forward!'

On 7 June 1944, the day after D-Day, Allied forces reaching the village of Turqueville, near Sainte-Mère-Église, accepted the surrender of a company of Georgian soldiers wearing the uniforms of the Wehrmacht. They interrogated the company's commander, Oberleutnant Lomtatidse, who told them that this was the 4th Company of the 795th Georgian Battalion. It is likely that these were the very first Georgian troops to fall into the hands of the Western Allies, and the interrogation record of Lomtatidse is quite revealing.[1]

He was described as 'a regular Russian [sic] Officer forced by starvation to join the Georgian Legion', according to his interrogation report. Previously, Lomtatidse had been an officer of the 646th Infantry Regiment in the 152nd Infantry Division of the Red Army when he was captured by the Germans in the battle for Smolensk in August 1941. The city of Smolensk had fallen to the Germans in July, so Lomtatidse had almost certainly participated in a failed Soviet counter-offensive to retake the town.

He somehow survived eight months of captivity during the first winter of the war on the Eastern Front – a time when Soviet prisoners were dying in their thousands of starvation and cold – and was taken away, together with eighteen other Red Army officers, all of them Georgians, to a prisoner of war camp in Zamostye, near Warsaw. It was then April 1942. As his interrogators summed up his story,

> Here about 1,000 starving Georgians were paraded. The German officers ordered all enemies of the Reich to step

forward. Nobody stepped forward since this would have meant a bullet in the neck. It was then announced that the ceremony of induction into the German Army was concluded.

Nearly all the Georgians who wound up wearing German uniforms had similar experiences.

One of the first to be captured was Valiko Zhgenti. He was taken prisoner by the Germans in Riga, the Latvian capital, in July 1941, at the very beginning of the German war with the Soviet Union and a month before Lomtatidse fell into German hands. Zhgenti had volunteered to serve in the Red Army, and he claimed that after his capture he escaped three times from custody – but never got very far. 'I was severely beaten for my efforts,' he said. 'The conditions in the camps were so bad that we even eat [sic] any dogs we managed to catch.'[2] He had become a captive of the Germans at the worst possible time, facing imprisonment during the winter of 1941–2, when conditions were unimaginably bad for the Soviet prisoners.

Noe Gongladze was also captured during those first few weeks of the fighting as the German forces mounted their *Blitzkrieg* against the Soviet Union. He was twenty-nine when he was badly injured on 20 August 1941 and taken by the Germans to a camp near Minsk; they refused to treat his wounds. The following month, his group was brought to Warsaw, but by then half of the prisoners had died. In the end, he said, the death toll reached 80 per cent.

Shalva Loladze was a captain who commanded a squadron in the Soviet Air Force. He was shot down in 1942 over occupied Ukraine and captured by the Germans. He eventually joined the Georgian Legion and was given the rank of *Leutnant* (second lieutenant).[3]

Another of the Georgians captured by the Germans was Evgeni Artemidze. We know more about his recruitment and experience in the Legion because he survived the war to talk about it. According to his daughter Gulia Artemidze, whom I interviewed in Georgia, Evgeni served in the Red Army in an artillery unit, and was captured after having served in Ukraine. In the German prisoner of war camp in Romania, he was near death and delirious when he heard someone calling out, asking if there were any Georgians in the camp. He thought it was a dream at first. Artemidze was recruited to the Georgian Legion by Georgian émigrés, among them General Kvinitadze, who were travelling from one prisoner of war camp to another, searching out Georgians willing to don German uniforms.[4]

Varlam Lomidze joined the Red Army in March 1942. He was a history teacher in Tbilisi at the time. Like many other Georgian soldiers, he was sent to fight in Crimea where he was captured by the Germans. He was forced to march some 800 kilometres to Zhitomir, a city to the west of Kiev in Ukraine, together with 20,000 other prisoners, suffering from hunger the whole way.

Zhgenti, Gongladze, Loladze, Artemidze and Lomidze all wound up in the 822nd Battalion.

As Gongladze recalled, in January 1943: 'The Germans brought those of us who could still walk to Kruszyna,' a town in southern Poland. He had already survived seventeen months in German captivity. He and the others were recruited to the Georgian Legion which was then being formed. As he described the recruitment, 'Those who refused to put on a German uniform were shot immediately.' His story is very similar to the one told by Lomtatidse to his Allied captors in France in 1944.

> Anything was better than being shot. Our intention was to wait until the injured had regained their strength and we had [to] have weapons. We were waiting to seize the right opportunity. It was here that I got to know Loladze ... We swore that we have our revenge.[5]

One of the Germans assigned to work with the Georgians at the Kruszyna camp was Dieter Röhren. He said that there were about 3,000 Georgians and fifty Germans based there. New recruits were brought in all the time, still wearing their Red Army uniforms. In April 1943, about 1,000 of the Georgians were separated from the others and formed into a new battalion – the 822nd. They were moved to new camp in Dęblin, fifteen kilometres away.

Loladze was the commander of the third company in the battalion. Röhren had daily contact with him. He remembered that despite their many disagreements, there was mutual respect between the two men. 'In general,' he said, 'I could get along well with the Georgians. I was one of the few Germans who tried to learn their language. This was very handy as most of them did not speak any Russian.'[6]

The commander of the 822nd Battalion was First Lieutenant Klaus Breitner, who would accompany the Georgians on their journey from Poland to France, and then on to their final destination on Texel. Breitner was interviewed about the formation of his battalion decades after the war, and dismissed stories that the men were somehow forced to enrol. 'Prisoners of war entered the German Army voluntarily,' he said. 'It was not a matter of necessity or pressure.'[7]

But Allied sources disagree. According to a British War Office report at the time,

> Starvation was the prime factor in recruiting ex-Soviet soldiers for the 'Russian Army of Liberation' and the various other Eastern Legions. Canteens at prisoner of war camps for captured Soviet soldiers sold human flesh of [the] recently deceased to hungry Soviets.[8]

After their 'ceremony of induction', those men who did not step forward and declare their enmity to Reich were made to sign a declaration which committed them to the following:

> To be honest, to work conscientiously, to fulfil all orders received from one's commanders, to love Hitler and to work sincerely for Germany. He who breaks the above undertaking becomes an enemy and will be severely punished.

The officers who administered the oath warned the Georgians that failure to sign it was a death sentence. As the Allied interrogation report concluded, 'Everybody signed.'

For the first four months after the 'induction' the new Georgian recruits to the Wehrmacht underwent training in Vesola, a village in Poland. This included tactics, drill, physical training and 'political education'. The group was commanded by a German officer, Hauptmann Kuseleff, who worked together with Breitner. The German officers were assisted by General Shalva Maglakelidze who was well known to many of the Georgians.

Born in 1893, Maglakelidze was educated in a Georgian high school in Kutaisi, a city to the west of the capital. He eventually obtained a doctorate in law in Berlin. During the First World War, he served in the Russian Army. He supported Georgian independence when it was declared in 1918, but he did not like the ruling Social Democrats and their republic. He preferred a monarchy and thought it best for a German prince to take the Georgian throne. But he loyally served as a general in the Georgian Army until it was defeated in 1921 by the Soviets. He went into exile after the Soviet invasion, later living in Riga. A lifelong Germanophile, Maglakelidze grew close to Friedrich Werner von der Schulenburg, who was the last German commander of the Georgian Legion during the First World War.

The Germans eventually agreed to establish a second incarnation of the Georgian Legion. That legion had the political support of some of the Georgian exiles, particularly the ones based in Germany. As an Allied intelligence report from 1944 described it:

> The Georgian Legion is sponsored by a Georgian National Committee resident in Berlin. This Committee has an offshoot in Paris. Both bodies have the primary duty of publishing Georgian newspapers and supervising the political outlook within the Legion. The National Committee has no administrative power. This is held exclusively by the Legion Headquarters. The National Committee was most instrumental during the recruiting phase of the Georgian Legion; however its present importance is merely political and does not affect the military picture.
>
> The Georgian Legion Headquarters is located at Castres (Pyrenees) where the Headquarters controls a large replacement and training camp. In addition, the Legion controls, administratively at least, eight Georgian Legion battalions in the Field. Operationally, the regular battalions are controlled by the larger German formation to which they are assigned.

Colonel Machts commands the Georgian Legion and is directly responsible to the General of Volunteer Formations, Koestring.

However, the numbering operationally is so arranged as to fall into line with the German system of numbering Eastern Troops. The first Georgian Battalion is also the 795 Georgian Infantry Battalion. The battalions are numbered in a straight block from 795–802 (802 Georgian Infantry Battalion being also the 8th Georgian Battalion of the Georgian Legion).[9]

The captured Georgian officer Lomtatidse added more details, noting that 'The Berlin committee published a Georgian newspaper "Sakartvelo" and the Paris committee published one called "Legionnaire".' Lomtatidse insisted 'that corruption in these committees was considerable. Committee members received a salary of 500 marks monthly and in addition were granted a car and a house. . . . Apparently the Paris committee was considerably less Germanophile than its Berlin counterpart.' That may have been the case because of the involvement of the exiled Social Democrats, who were based near Paris.

The Allies received a picture of low morale among the Georgian legionnaires. Lomtatidse was reported to be 'exceedingly emotional on this subject'. He insisted that the Georgians were 'not animated by hostility to the USSR and that if they were assured of an amnesty they would not fight at all'. The Germans had been telling Georgians that at the end of the war – if Germany were to lose – all the Georgian prisoners of war would be automatically handed over to the Soviets and shot.

It is interesting to note that this was what the Germans were telling their Georgian troops in June 1944 or earlier, even though it was only at Yalta in 1945 that a final decision was announced by the Allied leaders to repatriate Soviet citizens – troops, prisoners of war, and forced labourers – who were found in Germany.

Some of the Georgian troops, Lomtatidse said, might well be willing to fight against the Allies as they 'still imagine they have nothing to lose by resisting'.

Not all the information Lomtatidse provided was accurate, but some of the rumours were interesting in their own right. For example, he believed that Stalin's son, Yakov, who had been captured by the Germans 'is serving as an officer in the legion'. (He wasn't.) He also reported the rumour that the son of Soviet foreign minister Molotov had been recruited to the newly formed 'Russian Liberation Army' of General Vlasov.

From late 1943 until the end of the war, the Georgians – having been taken far away from the Eastern Front where they may have been tempted to rejoin their former comrades in the Red Army – were mostly deployed on anti-invasion duty in France and elsewhere along Hitler's 'Atlantic Wall'.

The captured Georgian legionnaires liked to portray themselves as guards, or people involved in construction of defences, and not as combatants. And yet there were stories of some Georgians acting as enthusiastic allies of the Germans. For example, in Brittany there are reports that Georgian soldiers gouged out the eyes of French partisans. When these Georgians were captured by Free French troops in August 1944, they were summarily executed for this crime.[10]

As Donald Rayfield summed it up, there are 'a number of references to Georgian militia's pro-German atrocities, e.g. in the 1944 Vercors rebellion... There is material on Georgian collaborators in the Ministry of Interior archives in Tbilisi.' But on the whole, he wrote, the men serving in the Georgian Legion 'were victims, in that the alternative for them was starving to death in the Stalags'. Rayfield is convinced that 'Very few actively supported the allies until it was obvious they were going to be captured by them and would need to earn merit.'[11]

For the most part, the Georgians serving in the German armed forces did so involuntarily and without great enthusiasm. Sometimes, as we shall see in the next chapter, they proved to be very unreliable allies.

Chapter 6

Unreliable Allies

At one of his situation conferences on 12 December 1942 at the *Wolfsschanze* (Wolf's Lair), Hitler lectured his generals on the subject of the Georgians. There had been some discussion about the possible formation of German Army units consisting of Georgians and other Soviet peoples. Collectively these former Red Army soldiers now in German captivity would be known as *Osttruppen* (Eastern Troops) once they put on German uniforms.

> The Georgians don't belong to the Turkish peoples [Hitler explained]. The Georgians are a Caucasian tribe that has nothing to do with the Turkish peoples. I regard only the Muslims as safe. All the others I consider unsafe. That can happen to us anywhere, so we have to be incredibly cautious. For the time being, I regard the building up of these pure Caucasian nations as quite risky, whereas I don't see a danger in building up a unit consisting of only Muslims.
>
> [The Georgians make] themselves available to all sides … they are, according to what we hear, quite unreliable to all sides. However I can imagine that because Stalin himself is a Georgian, quite a lot of people are attracted to the Communists. They had a kind of autonomy … The Georgians are not a Turkish people, rather a typical Caucasian tribe, probably even with some Nordic blood in them. Despite all explanations – either from Rosenberg or from the military side – I don't trust the Armenians, either. I consider the Armenian units to be just as unreliable and dangerous. The only ones I consider to be reliable are the pure Muslims, which means the real Turkish nations.[1]

Hitler may have had a point. Some of the Georgians who wound up serving in the Wehrmacht turned out to be rather less reliable allies of Nazi Germany than had been hoped. As the war raged on, the number of incidents of desertion and mutiny increased. The events on Texel in April 1945 may be seen as a culmination of that process.

The problems started early, when the first Georgian recruits began their training. According to an Allied intelligence report, 'The legionaries were equipped with Russian weapons, but as there were many cases of desertion and of arms being smuggled to Polish partisans, the Germans insisted on all weapons being returned at the conclusion of a day's training.'

Even the élite Bergmann Battalion, comprised of volunteers, suffered from desertions. As one historian put it,

> There were instances of desertions in the 'Tamar - 2' and 'Dromedar' Abwehr groups that speak about the poor state of the psychological and ideological training of the volunteers, although in the beginning of the campaign against Russia, the situation vis-à-vis the national legions was worse.[2]

Aware of the growing problem, the Germans 'periodically conducted ideological training classes and the occasional purging of "untrustworthy legionary elements" within the formations.'[3] But these were no more successful than the ideological education and purges that characterised the Red Army in which these men had already served. If political commissars from the Communist Party had failed to 'educate' these men, the Nazi propagandists would later have no better luck.

The Germans were right not to trust their new Georgian recruits, despite their having signed that oath to 'love Hitler' and 'work sincerely for Germany'. (After all, they had previously made similar commitments to Stalin and the Soviet Union.)

By August 1942, the first Georgian soldiers were deployed to the Caucasus for anti-partisan work. Things did not go well. 'During this period,' according to captured Georgian officer Lomtatidse, 'individual desertions increased.' Early in 1943, half of the 2nd Georgian Battalion defected back to the Soviets and a similar thing happened within the

1st Battalion. As a result of this, the 2nd Battalion was disbanded and its personnel distributed elsewhere. In March 1943, the 1st Battalion was withdrawn from the region entirely.

The records of interrogations of captured soldiers from the Georgian Legion which are held in the National Archives in Kew contain a number of similar stories.

In early June 1944, British interrogators learned from a captured soldier from the Georgian Legion that after his battalion was deployed to the north Caucasus in September 1942, half of the battalion surrendered to the Soviets. In addition, he claimed, forty-eight men were sent to prison and the senior officer was shot.[4] Another captured Georgian soldier, Michail Mamiev, from the 795th Battalion, told his interrogators that he personally killed several Germans and defected to the Allied forces with some 200 other men. He claimed that smaller groups deserted from all the other companies.[5] A captured Georgian soldier from the 822nd Battalion, S. Elbakidze, told the British officers that his unit was deployed against partisans in the Briansk sector in the German-occupied area of Russia – but 'owing to large scale desertions [they] were transferred to France'.[6]

The Georgians having displayed a notable lack of enthusiasm on the Caucasian front as well as a tendency to desert, the Germans felt that it might be best to deploy them against partisans elsewhere. The highest-ranking Georgian officer, General Maglakelidze, had quickly fallen out of favour and was replaced by a German. Maglakelidze had opposed the deployment of the Georgians to fight on other fronts against partisans. He preferred that they be used in the fight against the hated Soviet regime. According to one account, he was court-martialed for calling a German officer 'a bandit'.

According to Lomtatidse's account, during their time battling Polish partisans Georgian 'desertions were considerable'. In October 1943, the Germans now 'found it unwise' to employ units of former Soviet POWs anywhere near the Eastern Front. The Georgians were deployed to France, the Netherlands and even the British Channel Islands.

In general, he reported that by this point 'relations between the Georgians and the Germans are not cordial and Georgian officers are not involved in important conferences. Suspicion between individual officers was considerable, through mutual fear of espionage.' As we know, the NKVD had put a number of its agents in place inside the Legion to subvert and disrupt its activities.

The Germans had growing doubts about their Georgian and other Soviet 'allies' and one indication of this was the decision late in the war to move some of the Georgian troops who had been stationed in Guernsey to the tiny island of Sark, where it was felt there was less risk of trouble.

While there were cases of individual Georgians defecting to the Allied side, there don't seem to be many examples of entire Georgian units turning on their German masters, especially once they had been deployed to the West. The story of Hirson, a town on the French side of the border with Belgium, is therefore an interesting one, as it foreshadows what would happen on Texel a few months later. The story is told in an unpublished memoir held by the Imperial War Museum in London.[7]

Christian de Groote, a Resistance member, recalled that while cycling on a road in August 1944 he suddenly came upon a group of German soldiers who jumped out of a wood to stop him: 'I saw immediately that they were in fact Georgians who, having become prisoners of war, had agreed to enrol in the German army. On the left sleeve of their uniform a little Georgian flag with the inscription "Georgia" made it possible to identify them.'

He knew that a group of Georgians serving in the German Army had been based in the old barracks of the Garde Mobile in Hirson. He noted their reputation: 'Efficient and zealous, they were renowned for their toughness and brutality.'

He was not happy that they ordered him to abandon his bicycle and follow them into the forest. They searched him thoroughly, and (to his surprise) took nothing. 'Not even my mother's chocolates,' he remembered. They kept asking him, in poor German, if he had seen any German soldiers. It made no sense to him at all. They were wearing German uniforms at the time. And then they let him go. He could not understand what had happened.

Later, he met a colleague, Ducrocq, who explained what had happened. 'A group of Georgians from Hirson, after killing their German officers, had fled into the forest, and somehow had made contact with the French Resistance,' he learned.

> Ducrocq wanted to meet and negotiate with them and try to win them over. We wanted their weapons (because we were almost without any), and they urgently required civilian clothes, and it was easy to understand why. I wasn't present when the bargaining took place, but it concluded in an agreement by which the Georgians were to give us their aid, and half their weapons, and receive civilian clothes.

De Groote then went with Ducrocq into the forest, where they were surrounded by about thirty of the Georgians. Some of them recognised him from their earlier encounter. 'Why didn't you tell us?' they said.

It was decided to put the Georgians in a hut which had previously been used by the Boy Scouts. It seems that there were about thirty Georgian soldiers in the group, and they were led by the French partisans through the woods, marching single file, towards the hut. De Groote wrote that he walked at the back of the group, and could still remember vividly those Georgians in their German battle uniforms and the sound their boots made in the forest.

> We took great care when crossing the road between Macquenoise and Saint-Michel, throwing ourselves to the other side, one by one, at the double. Finally, the hut, which proved to be big enough, was reached. I was then better able to take a good look at my new companions in arms and with their noses like the beaks of eagles, wild eyes (mostly black) they brought to mind birds of prey and were not lacking in bearing.

The leader of the Georgian group was a former lieutenant in the Red Army named Vladick Kacharava, and he had 'undisputed authority' among these men, who were completely loyal to him. De Groote, who knew some German, became the contact point between the French resistance and the Georgians, whose German was very poor – and whose French was presumably non-existent. The Georgians were left in the hut and a couple of French partisans chose the foot of a large tree as their base. De Groote went back to the hut later on to check on the Georgians.

It turned out that the Georgians had stopped three young women on a road. The women claimed to be smugglers crossing the Franco-Belgian border. They begged to be set free, claiming that their parents would be worried. De Groote told the Georgians to hold them as prisoners.

Later, there were reports of some German soldiers walking along the road, towards Belgium. De Groote was handed a revolver and went out with some of the Georgians to see what was going on. They spotted two Germans. The Georgians broke into two groups and then surrounded the Germans, who surrendered. De Groote felt sorry for the German soldiers, as they seemed terrified and helpless. They expected to be shot, he remembered, and the Georgians handled them quite roughly. De Groote told the Germans not to worry, and calmed down the angry Georgians. 'They were not very young and they did not appear to be swaggering Nazis,' he recalled. They brought the Germans back to the hut. The Germans had their boots confiscated, but no other harm came to them. It may have been because of the presence of the French Resistance fighters that the Georgians showed such restraint, for as we shall see when we reach the uprising on Texel, this would not always be the case.

Later in the day, the men were brought food, including cherry cake. The German prisoners were fed the same as the French partisans. In exchange, one of the German soldiers took out a box of cigars, which had somehow not been confiscated earlier, and offered cigars to all the men. It was a gesture of reconciliation that De Groote never forgot.

As for the three young women held by the Georgians, it turned out all right in the end. The girls were released, but seemed in no hurry to leave. They and some of the young Georgians had managed to become friendly.

Then the Georgians with their French Resistance allies took to the road again, this time marching to the village of Saint-Michel, which had already been abandoned by the retreating German forces.

One of the jobs given to the Georgians, who were now a part of the Free French forces, was to arrest three young women in a bistro, who had been accused of having slept with Germans during the occupation. This scene was to repeat itself across Europe as the war came to an end.

A high-ranking French Army officer eventually arrived and questioned De Groote about the Georgians. Meanwhile, the two German prisoners were given work: they peeled potatoes at a local farmhouse. The Georgians spent their time playing cards. In conversations with De Groote, the Georgians insisted on their love of Stalin and of Communism. Later, on Texel, many of the Georgian rebels would make the same claims.

The Georgian commander Kacharava asked for certificates from the resistance to prove that he and his men had helped the Free French. De Groote later heard that they had received just such a document from General de Gaulle. Again, this was part of a regular pattern, and the Georgians on Texel would also ask for, and receive, documents from the local Communist Party attesting to their heroic fight against the fascists.

The two German prisoners were eventually transferred to a POW camp. The Georgians had their weapons taken away from them, and were sent to one of France's Mediterranean ports and then repatriated to the Soviet Union via the Black Sea port of Odessa. As De Groote later heard, 'On disembarking in the USSR, they had all been shot without trial.'[8]

That may not have been the case, as we shall later see. Sometimes there were rumours like this, but the men who had been 'shot without trial' turned up alive and well years later. Of course the Stalinist regime did punish large numbers of men who had served the Germans, and even men whose only crime was to be captured by the Wehrmacht and held as prisoners of war. But not all of them were to suffer this fate.

The Georgians were not the only former Soviet soldiers serving in the German Army, and they were not the only ones to become increasingly unreliable allies. There were a number of examples of former Soviet soldiers turning on their German allies in the months before the uprising on Texel. On the last Sunday of August 1944, in the eastern part of France, another group of former Soviet prisoners, also dressed in German uniforms, would follow the same route of resistance as the Georgians of Hirson.[9]

This time, it was a battalion of Ukrainian soldiers who had been brought into a division of the Waffen-SS consisting of Russians, Armenians, Tatars and Belorussians. The Ukrainian officers had decided that, with the defeat of Nazi Germany in sight, it was time to rebel. They got in touch with a local French Resistance (Forces Françaises de l'Intérieur – FFI) commander, Simon Doillon, the owner of a local dairy.

Doillon laid down three conditions for the cooperation of the FFI with the Ukrainians. In exchange for providing shelter and other kinds of assistance, the Ukrainians first of all had to carry out the mutiny themselves, without any help from the French partisans. Second, once they had rebelled they would fall completely under the command of the FFI. Third, they were to liquidate the German commanders and take no prisoners. The last of these demands was quite different from the what the FFI in Hirson had suggested, but it was to become the norm in rebellions of this type, as we shall see in Texel the following year.

For that reason, it was becoming safer for a German soldier to be captured by the advancing Western Allies than it was to be exposed to the wrath of rebelling 'Eastern Troops' wearing Wehrmacht uniforms. As we shall see, some German soldiers requested to be transferred away from the untrustworthy *Osttruppen* to the safety of regular Germany Army units.

On the day of the mutiny, the Ukrainian soldiers and their German commanders were marching along a paved road. It was a hot day, and the column was moving quite slowly. Around mid-morning, the most senior of the Ukrainian officers, Major Lev Holba, was unsure if his men would follow his lead, and if they would have the courage to take on the Germans. But it was time to find out.

Holba nodded to one of his men and a flare was fired into the sky. Only a few of the Ukrainians understood what the signal meant. One of the them, a lieutenant, shouted out an order in their language – 'Helmets in place!' The Ukrainians followed the order and put on their helmets. An SS officer, Obersturmführer Bentz, riding on a horse next to the lieutenant, while not understanding the language got the gist of the order, and began to put on his helmet. The lieutenant turned to him and shot him in the head. The mutiny had begun.

The other Ukrainians understood what was happening and followed their officers' example. What happened next has been described as 'a wild storm of hand-to-hand combat to the death', with Germans being killed in many cases by rifle butts smashing into their skulls. The fighting lasted less than an hour. Hundreds of Germans were killed, among them twenty-five SS officers. The Ukrainians had lost only one man, and six were injured, two of whom later died from their wounds.

As a result of their bloody rebellion, they were ceremonially welcomed into the FFI that very evening. For weeks afterward, they continued to serve in the French resistance, providing assistance not only to the British Special Operations Executive (SOE) and the American Office of Strategic Services (OSS), but even to Stalin's NKVD, before participating in a final battle with the Wehrmacht.

These mutinies and defections, which began as soon as the Georgians started their training in 1942, can be seen as a warning to the German High Command that these men, many of whom had been given the choice in a prison camp of 'starve or fight', could not be trusted. It was a warning that largely went unheeded.

Eight months after the risings of the Georgians in Hirson and the Ukrainians in eastern France, and with the end of the war in sight, a far larger rebellion would take place in which many more lives would be lost.

Chapter 7

Texel in Wartime

'It Was All Very Amicable'

Texel is the largest and most populated of the West Frisian Islands in the Wadden Sea, just off the Dutch coast. It has just seven villages, the largest of which, in the centre of the island, is Den Burg. Like so much of the Netherlands, Texel's geography has been shaped to a large degree by the people who inhabit it. Once two islands, it was linked by a raised area of sand and rocks. In the early 1600s, a dyke was built to connect the two islands, keeping the North Sea at bay. The northern part of Texel saw the creation of an area of lowland known as a *polder* that was no longer undersea, and was now protected from the sea by dykes. The island is criss-crossed with canals, and consists mostly of flat agricultural land. There are a few small woodlands.

Texel was an important part of the Third Reich's sprawling Atlantic Wall, which was heavily fortified to prevent any Allied landing in western Europe. Artillery positions were located at the northern and southern ends of the island. For this reason, there was a relatively large German military presence on the island.

During the war the islanders themselves did not suffer very much, or at least not nearly as much as other Dutch people did. They had plenty of food and their community remained intact with neighbours supporting each other. Texel even provided a haven for children from the mainland, who were sent there by their parents. The memoir of one of these children, Hans Verhoeven, is a superb source of information about life under the German occupation.

One islander recalled that life 'was actually very peaceful in the village' and that 'Food collections were organised to send bags of potatoes and food to Amsterdam by freight ship.' The people living on the Dutch mainland suffered terribly from hunger, particularly in the final winter of the war. But this was not the case on Texel. Another Texelian said that 'We never went hungry. There was always enough food. My mother baked bread of wheat that was grown and milled here on Texel. The bread was baked with that. People slaughtered their own pigs.'[1]

In addition to having enough food, the locals don't recall having a particular problem with the German occupiers, who though unwelcome didn't behave as they did elsewhere in Europe. One woman recalled that 'in the evening we swam in the harbour and the German soldiers just looked on. It was pleasant,' she said, but 'you didn't associate with them. But there was no hatred between us.'[2] Another islander said, 'In the bakery, for instance, three or four Germans had to help bake bread. They were all old people. The Germans weren't seen as locals, but it was all very amicable.'[3]

The German soldiers – and later, the Georgians who served with them – were tasked with guard duty, drilling, and maintaining the artillery batteries (though the last of these were under exclusive German control). From time to time, they would shoot at Allied aircraft flying overhead. The bodies of some of the Allied pilots whose planes were downed over or near Texel are today buried in Den Burg's cemetery.

Among the Germans serving on Texel, there was a division of labour: Navy personnel manned the batteries while the Army was in charge of the rest of the island. The Hotel De Lindeboom in the heart of Den Burg is where the German officers would meet up.

As elsewhere in the Netherlands, a number of local people welcomed the Germans and collaborated with them, joining the Nationaal-Socialistische Beweging in Nederland (Dutch National Socialist Movement), known as the NSB. It's estimated that about 7 per cent of Texel's small population supported the NSB, which had been founded in the 1930s and achieved only limited success until the German invasion – though in pre-war parliamentary elections it managed to win more votes than the Communist Party. During the war, it was the only legal political party in the Netherlands.

The NSB's founder and leader was Anton Mussert, and he visited Texel to open the group's headquarters in Den Burg, in a building which today is a café. Though the NSB eventually claimed over 100,000 members across the country, it was greeted with suspicion by most Dutch people, many of whom chose to support the various resistance organisations instead. Most local people on Texel kept their distance from the collaborators in the NSB.

A resistance movement in Texel began to form early on, and among the first to sign up were the Snoek brothers. 'Long before the war, Huug Snoek, a sailor, had developed a hatred for swastikas and came to blows with Hitlerite supporters in a German harbour,' according to historian Dick van Reeuwijk.[4] The commander of the resistance on Texel was Wim Kelder, who had been a senior municipal official. Kelder's deputy was Jacob Keijzer, who remembered those early months of the war:

> In the beginning of the war, everything was rather quiet. The local people are easy-going and didn't have too many problems with the Germans. But of course, the Germans had no business being here. Our boys didn't want to remain passive for long, and on one occasion, they stole a couple of pistols from the Germans who were watching a film in the cinema. Actually, this was against instructions. The region commander of the Resistance in Alkmaar (on the mainland) wanted the situation on Texel to remain calm. This was because people on the run from the Germans were hiding on Texel and one drawback of being on an island is, of course, that escaping is difficult once you've been discovered.[5]

Early on, locals spoke about their fears that the war might perhaps end quickly with a German victory, especially if the Americans stayed out. There was some concern that if this happened, the NSB might be able to seize power. As Keijzer put it, 'We decided that we needed to have an organisation to resist them. And in the back of our mind we thought we might also have to take on the Germans some day. We established a complex, secret organisation which soon recruited about 400 people.'[6]

After just five days of fighting, the Dutch Army had surrendered to the Germans. Their queen, Wilhelmina, and her government fled to Britain. It took another couple of weeks for the first Germans to start arriving on the island. A quartermaster named Heinz Hlawatschek came over by ferry a week before the main body of German soldiers was due to arrive. His job was to find accommodation for those who would occupy the island. During a brief ceremony, the local Dutch commander, Captain Piet van der Linden, handed over the island to the Germans. When the ceremony ended, the two men headed over to the Hotel Texel for a drink.

Heinz Hlawatschek turned out to be an ally of the Dutch, an informant for the resistance throughout the war. He let the locals know when there would be arrests and searches:

> I maintained good contact with the locals from 1940 onwards. Due to my position as quartermaster, I was able to do things for people such as giving information when the situation became dangerous. As [a] result the relationship became closer and closer and has stayed that way ever since.[7]

Hlawatschek was also able to help the men who were smuggling food from Texel back to the mainland, and smuggling people who were hiding from the Germans back to Texel. He gave them directions which they followed. He recalled how the German occupation forces grew. 'In the beginning, there were only about 200 German soldiers on Texel,' he explained in an interview,

> This increased to 1,000 relatively quickly and by 1942 the garrison numbered around 2,000 men. As an integral part of the Atlantic Wall, Texel was quite well defended but the majority of the German Army stationed there had nothing to do with the defence of the island. Most of them were moved to Texel for a break from the front since it remained quiet here during the war.[8]

His description of most German soldiers being 'on a break' on Texel is confirmed by photographs, some in colour, now held by the island's archives. They show smiling German soldiers, sometimes with their girlfriends, playing sports and enjoying the good weather on the island. The Navy personnel in the coastal batteries occupied their time making handicrafts, playing games and holding swimming competitions. They preferred to swim in the nude. One of the Germans made a pair of water skis using part of a propeller from a downed aircraft. With little to do on the island other than wait for an Allied landing that would never come, the Germans published a little magazine. The southern battery even had its own small orchestra. They composed a song about their location on Texel, which included these lines:

> Far away from all culture,
> only between the dunes, the sand, and water,
> on the dunes one thing is certain,
> Humour is the very best cure.

When they were not busy relaxing and having fun, the Germans turned Texel into a fortress, with some 500 concrete bunkers constructed across the island. Many of them still exist. They also laid minefields along the coast, and strung up barbed wire to slow down any invading force.

The southern battery had artillery pieces with a range of 13.5 km, as well as anti-aircraft guns. It was surrounded by minefields and its perimeter was patrolled by sentries. The northern battery, which was swept away by the sea after the war, was officially known as Battery Eierland. The remaining fortifications were mostly on the North Sea coast, built of reinforced concrete and surrounded by minefields like the artillery positions. All the strongholds were given code names that began with the letter 'I' such as Infant, Irrtum, and Indien. The coastal batteries were manned by the German Navy; the other positions were held by Army personnel, including the Georgians.

The main bunker complex, known as Texla, was situated just outside the town of Den Burg. Others were located at Ongeren (its code name was Dora), at the airfield (code named Anton) and by the lighthouse (Bertha). The troops not sitting in the bunkers were kept in reserve both in Den Burg and by the airfield. The harbour in Oudeschild, which faced the Dutch coast, had anti-aircraft guns, operated by the Navy, as well as its share of bunkers.

While the Germans spent their time swimming and playing games, some of the population on Texel looked for ways to resist their rule. They decided early on to 'maintain the calm on Texel' and banned acts of sabotage. Instead of armed struggle against the Germans, they focussed on helping hide people who needed safe places to stay. They also monitored the activities of the fascist NSB. The deputy commander of the local resistance, Jacob Keijzer, was ordered by his superiors in Alkmaar to infiltrate the NSB:

> The circle commander asked if it would be possible for me to become a member of the NSB. Well, I had many acquaintances within the NSB, so that was no problem. So I told him that I could become the commander of the *Wehrabteilung* [WA – Defence Detachment] within a year and if required, I'd educate myself in Schalkhaar [the National Socialist movement's education centre in the Netherlands]. Then I would be the only NSB member on Texel with a degree.

But before Keijzer could begin his role as double agent, he was told to talk this over with his local priest, as he was a Catholic. And the priest warned him what might happen: 'You can't just do something like that. You mean it well, but I can't take responsibility for this – there are several Catholics on the [NSB] waiting list, asking themselves: shall we join or not?' As Keijzer remembered, 'The priest was concerned that many people would follow my example if I would appear in church in a WA uniform. He took the matter to the bishop, who was also totally opposed to it.'

The resistance leadership understood the problem, and despite Keijzer's belief that he could rise to the top of the NSB, he was told to pretend to be a sympathiser, nothing more. As he played an active role in the resistance on Texel, this led to some strange situations. 'Once during an underground meeting in my house,' he said, 'the editor of the NSB magazine *Volk und Vaterland* came by. The man stayed half the night, while members of the underground hid all over the house.' Keijzer managed to keep his cover throughout, and many of his NSB 'comrades' were astonished to see him honoured at the end of the war for his role in the resistance.

Though on the whole the people of Texel did not suffer nearly as much as people in other territories occupied by the Germans, on 10 November 1944 they did get a rude awakening. With no warning at all, the Germans ordered all men between the ages of seventeen and thirty-five to report to their command headquarters in Texla. To ensure that all the men did report, raids were carried out. No one seemed to know what was happening.

The men were taken off the island to the Dutch mainland. A group of 100 went first, followed by 500 and a final group of another 100. They were taken to Assen, a city in the north-eastern part of the Netherlands, to dig tank traps to block the advance of the Allied forces. Not all the men complied with the German order. Leo Smit was one of those. An activist in the farmers' union who had helped fugitives to hide, he did not report to Texla. Instead he hid in the cellar of the employment office in Den Burg, together with Tom Zwaard. There they were able to listen to the news on the BBC and produced forty-three editions of an underground newspaper, *De Aatherbode*.

After a few weeks shoring up the defences around Assen, the men of Texel returned to the island, no doubt unhappy with the German occupiers, who until that time had generally behaved correctly. In the deportation of the men as forced labourers to the mainland, they experienced another and much uglier side of the German occupation.

And it was soon to get far worse.

Chapter 8

The Georgians and the Dutch

Zandvoort

In early November 1942, the Allied victory in the second battle of El Alamein marked the beginning of the end of German hopes in North Africa, and in the eyes of some it was a turning point in the war. Winston Churchill famously said: 'Before Alamein we never had a victory. After Alamein, we never had a defeat.' A few months later, the battle of Stalingrad was over and German hopes of winning the war on the Eastern Front were gone. And by the early summer of 1943, Allied forces had landed in Sicily. There would be two more long years of fighting, but Axis armies were now in retreat on all fronts.

The former Red Army soldiers now serving in the *Ostlegionen* (Eastern Legions) would have known much of this, and some were certainly considering switching sides, in part to demonstrate their loyalty to Stalin and the Soviet Union as it was becoming clearer who would win the war. We don't know exactly when the Georgians serving in the 822nd Battalion came to the realisation that they were on the losing side in the war, but we do know that once they had transferred from Poland to France and then the Netherlands, an underground organisation had been created within their ranks.

The leaders of the group included Shalva Loladze, Sergei Gujabidze, and Evgeni Artemidze and by April 1944, a full year before the uprising on Texel, they had established contact with members of the Dutch Resistance. The connection with the underground was helped by a certain I. Bondarev, a former colonel of the tsarist army, who had remained in Holland after being captured by the Germans during the First World War.

In Zandvoort, a coastal town near Haarlem where the Georgians were now deployed, they made contact with a group of Dutch Communists led by Annie van Ommeren-Averink, who later became a member of parliament, and who was known to the resistance as 'Annie Klein'. The 31-year-old Communist was very active in the resistance in Haarlem, and had previously played a role in organising the famous *Februaristaking*, a general strike in February 1941, called by the Communist Party to protest the persecution of the Dutch Jews. The strike lasted for just two days, but eventually involved hundreds of thousands of Dutch workers. It was the only mass protest in Nazi-occupied Europe against the deportation of Jews, and it was crushed by the Germans. The deportations continued.

Annie Klein formed a strong bond with the Georgians, in particular with Artemidze.

The Georgians stole weapons, food and explosives from the Germans and passed them on to the Dutch resistance. They deactivated some coastal mines to make an Allied landing easier, whenever that might occur. They tried to send messages to Britain. As the relationship between the Georgians and the Dutch Communists deepened, a special issue of *De Waarheid* ('The Truth'), the illegal publication of the Communist Party was published for the Georgians.

They began to discuss an armed uprising against the Germans, and held a special meeting on the subject in the summer home of Mari Andriessen, in Haarlem. Annie Klein and Jan Brasser, the sabotage commander for North Holland, were there to discuss plans with the Georgians. Many years later, Brasser recalled the meeting:

> On that stormy evening at the end of 1944, Loladze, the commander of the Georgians, and Artemidze, the political leader, put forward a plan to march on Amsterdam. They were certain that the population would take their side. We had to argue for a long time to convince them that this was not feasible. It would have been an impossible task to fight the Germans with a small force of only 800 men. The Dutch population didn't have any weapons and the Allies were still too far away. It would have been an enormous bloodbath.[1]

It's important to note the timing of this discussion. Some historians have claimed that the Georgians eventually decided to rebel only in April 1945 because of their imminent redeployment to the mainland. But as Brasser and others have confirmed, they had actually begun plotting their mutiny many months beforehand. Brasser described how they changed the minds of Loladze and Artemidze and talked them out of a rebellion at that point:

> We recalled the tactics of the Russian partisans who caused enormous amounts of damage to the Wehrmacht by destroying supplies and making transports impossible. These partisans didn't start a rebellion against the entire German Army.

One wonders if anyone in the room understood the irony of this comparison. These men had just come over from the Eastern Front where they had been deployed in anti-partisan operations in Poland and, in some cases, in the Soviet Union itself. They were now being told to learn the tactics of the men against whom they had only recently been fighting. As Brasser remembered, 'Nevertheless, we told them that they had an opportunity to take revenge if the Germans deployed them against the Allies. After a long discussion, they agreed and postponed the rebellion pending the moment they were sent to the front.'[2]

There has been talk over the years – and this was part of the later Soviet mythology about the rebellion – that the Georgian soldiers on Texel were somehow non-combatants, or even unarmed prisoners of war, but this conversation shows (as does much else) that this was not the case at all. They clearly were armed and even had access to additional weapons which they were able to share with their Dutch comrades.

In Zandvoort, and then on Texel, the Georgians specifically sought out the Dutch Communists, expecting that they would find willing allies – despite the fact that the Georgians had twice betrayed the Soviet Union, first by surrendering and then by joining the German Army. But there is no evidence that the Dutch Communists considered any of this a problem. To the contrary, they welcomed collaboration with the Georgians because a Georgian uprising would solve a problem for them too.

The history of the Dutch Communists during the Second World War was in fact a complicated one, and they – no less than their new Georgian friends – needed to do some work on their reputation before the war came to an end. Why was this the case?

In many of the countries which fell under German rule during the Second World War, resistance movements sprang up which carried out daring acts of sabotage. Many leading fighters in those movements were Communists, and this was as true in the Netherlands as it was elsewhere. In some countries, Communist parties later used their record in the wartime resistance to win legitimacy and support they had lacked before the war. But that is not the whole story.

First of all, the strength of the Communist Parties varied considerably from country to country. The German Communist Party, the largest and most important one outside the Soviet Union prior to 1933, had been destroyed in the wake of Hitler's rise to power that year. And while large Communist parties existed in countries like France and Italy, in many other places the Communists were a tiny and marginal force.

This was the case in the Netherlands. The Communistische Partij Holland (CPH) had barely 10,000 members when the war broke out in 1939, and had won little more than 3 per cent of the vote in the Dutch elections of 1937. The local fascist party got more votes than that. The Communists were hardly a mass movement.

And the CPH's attitude toward the Germans, before and after the May 1940 invasion of the Netherlands, was guided entirely by the Moscow-based leadership of the Communist International (Comintern), as was the case for all Communist parties. The Comintern, an international organisation of Communist parties founded by Lenin in 1919, had evolved to become an arm of Soviet foreign policy. Its instructions were drafted in the Soviet capital and obeyed by loyal party members around the world.

When the Soviet leadership felt threatened by Nazi Germany during most of the 1930s, all the parties affiliated to the Comintern – including the CPH – took a hard line against the Nazis. At one point they pivoted left, denouncing the Social Democrats in every country as 'social fascists' and insisting that only they, the Communists, were true anti-fascists.

They later pivoted right, warning of the dangers of fascism, and called for a 'popular front' against the far right, joining coalitions with the same Social Democrats who only yesterday had been their sworn enemies.

Communist parties survived these zig-zags in policy with varying degrees of success. But the policy of slavishly following the Kremlin lead took a bizarre turn in August 1939 with the signing of the Hitler–Stalin Pact. The two countries, which had previously been sworn enemies, pledged not to invade each other (though the Germans had no intention of complying with this pledge). The Nazis, who only the day before had been the worst enemies of the Soviet Union were now, suddenly, Stalin's allies. For many Communists in many countries this was a step too far, and the parties lost a considerable number of members. Many others, however, remained in the Communist movement, trusting that Stalin and the Soviet leadership knew what they were doing.

The problem of the Hitler–Stalin Pact became acute once the Wehrmacht made its turn to the west in the spring of 1940. Suddenly Communist parties found themselves living under German occupation, at a time when Nazi Germany and the Soviet Union were allies.

In spite of the sharp turn in Soviet foreign policy, and following an initial period when the party leaderships were in disarray, Communist leaders in the Netherlands and elsewhere quickly followed the line laid down in Moscow. But they still attempted to demonstrate a degree of continuity with their previous policies. For example, they explained away the Second World War as a battle between two kinds of imperialism – the new fascist imperialism (Germany and Italy) and the old reactionary imperialism of the British, Dutch and French empires. Workers, they said, had no interest in either side winning.

There was a precedent for this, in a way. The founding generation of Communist leaders emerged out of the First World War as opponents of both sides in that conflict. Many of the traditional Social Democratic parties had decided to support their own governments in that war, most notably the German Social Democrats, betraying pre-war commitments to refuse to support any side in the upcoming war. The Social Democrats' betrayal of their internationalist values led many to leave those parties in disgust and to found the organisations which later became Communist parties. It was Lenin, then living in neutral Switzerland, who called upon the working classes of all European countries to 'turn the imperialist war into a civil war'.

The Communist leaders in 1940 struggled to convince anyone that Lenin's strategy from a quarter century earlier of 'revolutionary defeatism' (supporting the defeat of one's own capitalist government) made any sense under the new circumstances of a totalitarian Nazi regime. Obviously, living under a fascist regime was worse than living under a liberal capitalist one, as the Communists themselves had conceded during most of the 1930s, particularly in their advocacy of the popular front.

As for the Netherlands' own policy of neutrality, which had been brazenly violated by the Germans when they invaded in May 1940, the Dutch Communists denounced this as being 'hypocritical', insisting that the country was not genuinely neutral. One of the leaders of the Dutch Communists wrote that terms like 'fascism', 'bourgeois democracy', and even 'aggression' had lost their meanings. They certainly had for the Communists themselves, who struggled to come up with a language to explain their stance during the nearly two years of the Soviet–German alliance. Their main enemy remained at home – the Dutch capitalists and their government, who were propped up by the 'traitors' in the Sociaal-Democratische Arbeiderspartij (SDAP – the Social Democratic Workers' Party).

The Communist leaders claimed that the SDAP were 'advocates of Polish fascism, of the Polish great landowners and of the Polish anti-Semites' because they opposed the September 1939 invasion of Poland by both the USSR and Germany.[3] It's not entirely clear how the Polish people, and in particular the Jews of Poland, benefited from German fascists and German anti-semites replacing Polish ones, but this was the logical consequence of support for the Nazi–Soviet alliance.

The Dutch Communists accused the SDAP leaders of supporting the 'western imperialists'. They were outraged as well at the anti-Nazi stand of the International Federation of Trade Unions, which had been founded in Amsterdam after the First World War. (The Communists had their own international trade union organisation known as the

Profintern which was based in Moscow.) In addition to training their fire on the Dutch Social Democrats and trade unionists, the Communists were fiercely critical of the Norwegian Social Democrats for supporting resistance to the German invaders.

The days of the popular front when the Communists would call on their Social Democratic 'comrades' to join them in resisting fascism were now a distant memory. The Communists claimed that the Social Democrats, like the Dutch government, were only pretending to be neutral in the war, while in reality backing the British imperialists and thereby dragging the Netherlands unnecessarily into the conflict.

Still trying to retain something of their links to an earlier period, to justify their twists and turns, the Dutch Communists announced their expectation that in any case this war would lead to a disintegration of the capitalist system worldwide. But that was off in the distant future. In the here and now, the Dutch Communists decided that in the event of a German invasion, they would offer *no military resistance.*

The Dutch Army surrendered after just five days of fighting in mid-May 1940. The country fell under German occupation. Meanwhile, the Soviet Union remained a German ally. For the next thirteen months, the Dutch Communists found themselves in the unenviable position of having to focus their propaganda attacks against the British (and the Americans, who had not yet entered the war), rather than against the Germans. And while the German occupiers were busy imposing the horrors of Nazi rule on the country, the Communists there, as in other countries occupied by Germany, were treated with kid gloves.

The Dutch Communists missed out on the first period of the resistance and tried to make up for lost time once the Soviet Union had been invaded and they could resume their anti-Nazi work in the underground, from June 1941 onwards. When Annie Klein met up with the Georgians in 1944, it was part of an effort to get more proactive in the fight against the German occupier, and perhaps even to atone for the failure of her party back in 1940–1, when they were put in the position of collaborating with the fascists.

They would get their chance to fight the Germans by proxy in just a few weeks.

On Texel

The Georgians stayed in Zandvoort for only a few months, never realising any of the plans they made with Annie Klein and the Dutch Communists, including their ill-conceived dream of a march on Amsterdam. To men who had served on the Eastern Front, and then battled against partisans in the frozen forests of Poland, the tranquil island of Texel must have appeared to be a little paradise when the 822nd Battalion arrived there on 10 January 1945.

The 822nd Battalion came to replace a unit of North Caucasians – also former Red Army men – who were being redeployed to the mainland. Those North Caucasians had earlier replaced a group of Indians who had arrived on Texel in 1943, believing that the best way to fight for their country's independence from the British Empire was by joining the German side in the war.

On the day that the Georgians arrived on Texel, Evgeni Artemidze went to visit Jacob Keijzer, the deputy leader of the local resistance:

> a small Russian named Artemidze called to my home to establish contact. I didn't know this man at all. Of course, I was a little surprised, wondering how he knew my address. He told me 'comrades' gave him my name. He proposed we become friends before talking further.[4]

Keijzer raised an interesting question. How did Artemidze know the name and address of one of the local resistance leaders, and contact him so quickly? Presumably Annie Klein and the Dutch Communists were the source of his information. Artemidze was clearly able to roam the island freely without any fear of the Germans discovering what he was doing. This had also been the case earlier, during the Georgians' deployment in Zandvoort. At the very least, this activity belies the claim later made by Soviet propaganda that the Georgians were prisoners of the Germans. Prisoners do not visit resistance leaders in their homes and plot rebellions with them. As Keijzer recalled:

> After that, he came every evening to tell about their experiences in Poland, France and Zandvoort. He wanted to meet the

Resistance, but it soon became apparent to me that he valued the communist movement more than our group. I never really liked that.[5]

Keijzer was not a Communist, and there were hardly any Communists at all on Texel, but eventually Artemidze found someone who was. Cornelia Boon-Verberg lived near De Cocksdorp, close to the very northern tip of the island. She remembered first meeting the Georgians after they arrived on Texel:

> They dropped in to buy eggs, and tried to find any news from the front, and to find out what we thought of the Germans. I showed them a book with a picture of Stalin, and we were considered the best friends of the Soviet Union from then on. They kept in contact and after a while I found out what they were planning. I always knew there would be a moment when they would strike back at the Germans.[6]

Jacob Keijzer had a place to meet in a more central location, between the main town of Den Burg and the coastal town of De Koog. It was here that the Georgian leaders would convene secretly, away from the prying eyes of the Germans. There they even met one of the North Caucasians who had deserted from the German ranks and was hiding out in a house called 'Pomona', near the airfield. His name was Digurev.

Contact had been established with the mainstream resistance of which Keijzer was one of the leaders and with the local Communists, including Cornelia Boon-Verberg. And then nothing happened for nearly three months.

Artemidze and the others were growing impatient with their plans to stage an armed uprising. As Jacob Keijzer said,

> Artemidze came to my home in a highly nervous state in late March. He had to go to the mainland to inform the Communist Party about their plans. He said that there were about 16,000 Russians quartered along the coast up to the Hoek van Holland who would join the rebellion.[7]

Hoek van Holland (Hook of Holland) is a town in the south-western corner of the Netherlands. Artemidze was promising a rebellion that covered almost the entire coastline of the country. This sounded a lot like their earlier plan to march on Amsterdam, which the Dutch Communists had put a damper on.

It is not clear if Artemidze was consciously lying or just boasting to the Dutch resistance leader. There were thousands of former Soviet soldiers serving in the German Army in the Netherlands, but it is doubtful if the men on Texel were in direct contact with many of them. In the end, it turned out that the idea of a coordinated mass rebellion across many parts of the occupied Netherlands was a fantasy.

Like Annie Klein and Jan Brasser in Zandvoort a few months earlier, Keijzer splashed some cold water on Artemidze's plans: 'I said that the underground couldn't do anything without an order from England, but that it could be arranged.'[8]

It was starting to look like there was not going to be a Georgian uprising on Texel any time soon. And the war was rapidly coming to an end.

When one looks at the photographs German soldiers took of themselves on Texel, enjoying the sunshine and beaches, far from the front lines and in little danger of being bombed or shot at, one realises how lucky they were. Millions of their comrades were engaged in a life-or-death struggle on the Eastern Front against a rapidly advancing Red Army that showed little mercy to the German invaders who were now in retreat. Most of the rest of the German Army was fighting a losing battle against the advancing Allied armies in the west. Texel could have been described, as the British Channel Islands were by one Wehrmacht soldier, as a *'kleine Paradies'* ('little paradise').

A Georgian survivor who fought on Texel, Grisha Baindurashvili, recalled many years later that 'The Dutch girls would dance Georgian dances with us. There was love and sympathy between us and the Dutch girls. The Dutch people told us that the Germans had ordered them to stay away from us, because we were cannibals.' As we saw earlier, this was a common theme in Nazi propaganda, depicting starving Soviet prisoners of war as sub-human cannibals. The Dutch clearly didn't buy it. 'We made friends with them,' he recalled.[9]

Marianne Bonne, from Texel, confirmed his account. 'They sometimes came along for a coffee or a chat. My aunt told me that she played boardgames with them. They were just young guys looking for something to do. And that's how it happened that my mother had an affair with him. My mother probably wasn't happy with my father, or this wouldn't have happened. I was born out of that affair.'[10]

She was not the only child born to a Georgian father following their short stay in the island. Decades after the war ended, islanders still suggest that there were a number of children born shortly after the war with distinctively Georgian features. One woman even claimed to be the daughter of the Georgian commander, Shalva Loladze.[11]

'The Dutch hated the German and so did we,' said Grisha Baindurashvili. 'The Dutch really hated them. That's why they respected us.'[12]

Dutch survivors from that period recall their often strange encounters with the Georgians. The Georgian troops:

> were putting posts in everywhere to prevent parachutists from landing. I was eleven and hanging around, because I was curious about these ferocious men. I was walking on the dyke and this Russian knelt down before me with tears in his eyes and he kissed me. I found it interesting, but also a bit scary. Out of his pocket he took a picture of a girl like me with long black braids. I understood then that he had a daughter my age.[13]

A man from Texel recalled the difficulties of communicating with the Georgians. 'Those guys tried to talk to you,' he said:

> Some spoke a bit of French, but we didn't. Some spoke a bit of German. We understood that reasonably well. They asked where you lived. They practised in the woods. A troop of about twenty-five would walk through the woods singing in four-part harmony.[14]

Like soldiers everywhere, the Georgian soldiers enjoyed the odd drink – or perhaps a bit more than that. As one women recalled, 'I remember that one shop sold methylated spirits. They bought that as well. And you know what? They drank it! They probably didn't get enough schnapps. They enjoyed their liquor, but we hardly noticed.'[15]

Another woman recalled how one of the Georgian soldiers became a friend of her family. She remembered a conversation with her mother:

> I said: 'Mum, there's a soldier in the shop.' She said: 'That's a Russian.' I went into the shop to have a look, but he seemed like an ordinary man. My mother said: 'He won't leave. He's been there for an hour.' We went to have our meal. My father came out of the bakery and said: 'Marie, give him a glass of milk, because this has to stop.' That's exactly what that boy wanted. He was called inside and sat down at the table. My mother gave him milk. We started to eat and he kept sitting there. When my smaller siblings had to go to bed at 7 p.m., he said: 'I want to come along.' So he helped putting the kids to bed.[16]

But one man recalled something else about the Georgians, who were often portrayed as singing, drinking, missing their children and flirting with the local women. The Georgians also seemed to have secrets, as one local recalled:

> From our house we could see the school playground where the Georgians were practising throwing hand grenades. We were laughing, because those guys handled the grenades in such a stupid and clumsy manner. In hindsight, they were putting on an act. They didn't display what they were capable of. I think they were trying to fool the Germans.[17]

Hans Verhoeven had this memory of the Georgians from before the uprising:

> In our foraging trips we met many 'Russians', as everyone called the Georgians. They were friendly and offered us lifts on their horse-drawn wagons. When you're walking with a pillowcase full of beans on your back such an invitation is very tempting but we never accepted. After all, they were in German uniform and their wagons carried German Nazi slogans in large white letters such as '*Glauben, Kämpfen, Siegen* [Believe, Fight, Win]'. Although they were dressed like German soldiers the Russians looked different. They had darker complexions, their hair, which

was usually black, was cut differently, and many had moustaches. They wore little shields with '*Georgien*' on their helmets and on the sleeves of their jackets. What little contact we had with them was – before the mutiny – a sporadic and shy acknowledgment of their greetings.

By April 1945, with the end of the war rapidly approaching, nearly everyone on Texel looked forward to the coming of peace. Eventually the Germans would surrender, their soldiers would go home to their families, and the Dutch civilians could resume the lives that were interrupted by the German invasion five long years before.

Everyone, that is, except for the Georgian soldiers of the 822nd Battalion. For them, the end of the war would not necessarily mean a happy reunion with their families. They were acutely aware of the fact that Stalin had twice sentenced them to death – with the infamous order which forbade them to surrender to the enemy in the first place, and of course following their decision to don German uniforms and to support the Nazi war effort.

They were also aware that the Western Allies who would soon take control of Texel as they chased the Germans out of the Netherlands were obligated by decisions taken by their leaders at Yalta to repatriate to the Soviet Union any captured Soviet citizens, including Red Army men who had surrendered or defected and who now wore the uniform of the hated German Army. They knew this because the Germans made certain they knew it. The Georgians serving on Texel could expect no sympathy when they returned home.

Keijzer recalled his late March meeting with Artemidze, with his grandiose plans to stage an uprising of Soviet troops across the Netherlands, from Texel down to Hoek van Holland. 'We didn't know the details of the Georgian plan for Texel,' he said, 'but I thought they would probably pick May 1 to launch the revolt.'[18]

Actually, it was going to come a whole lot sooner than that.

The swastika flag flying over Den Burg, Texel's main town.

One of the 500 bunkers constructed by the Germans on Texel.

Former Indian Army soldiers who had been persuaded to serve in the Wehrmacht were based on Texel before the Georgians arrived.

The Hotel de Lindeboom, in the centre of Den Burg, the *de facto* headquarters of the German occupation forces.

A German soldier on Texel relaxing with local women.

German personnel enjoying themselves on Texel.

A German serviceman having a snooze on the peaceful island.

German naval artillerymen receiving rations on Texel.

Germans keeping fit by playing games on Texel.

Members of the Georgian Legion of the Wehrmacht on parade.

Georgian soldiers of the 822nd Eastern Battalion relaxing on Texel.

Local Dutch Nazis on Texel. During the rising the Georgians wanted them all to be killed, but the Dutch resistance refused to allow this.

Above: Shalva Loladze, commander of the Georgian troops on Texel and leader of the uprising.

Right: Two wounded Georgian soldiers on Texel.

The bloodstained map of Texel that was used by the Georgian commander, Shalva Loladze.

The lighthouse on Texel where the Georgians made their last stand. It has since been rebuilt.

The Georgian Military Cemetery on Texel, 2018.

Poster for *Crucified Island*, the Soviet feature film about the uprising on Texel.

Below left: The memorial for Cornelia Boon-Verberg, the 'mother of the Georgians', in the Georgian cemetery on Texel.

Below: The grave of Evgeni Artemidze, a leader of the Georgian uprising on Texel, in Manglisi, Georgia.

Chapter 9

Day of Birth

By the beginning of April 1945, it was clear that Germany had lost the war. Soviet troops were about to take Vienna, Frankfurt/Main had been liberated, and German forces in the Ruhr were surrounded. In just two weeks, the battle for Berlin would begin.

In the Netherlands, British and Canadian divisions were racing across the eastern part of the country as they drove toward the German frontier. On 5 April Canadian troops captured the Dutch town of Almelo, 147 km south-east of Texel. Half of the Netherlands had now been liberated. Texel and the other Wadden Islands remained in German hands, but far from the front lines and strategically irrelevant as the fighting moved towards the Reich.

Major Klaus Breitner, commander of the 822nd Battalion, received an order to deploy four companies – about half of his Georgian troops – to the mainland. They were to join the desperate fight against the Allies, who were now moving to take Arnhem. Arnhem, near the German border, was the scene of the previous year's Operation Market Garden, Field Marshal Bernard Montgomery's bold but unsuccessful attempt to bring the war to an early conclusion. Now, six months later, the British were back and the German Army was in full retreat. Arnhem would soon be liberated after five years of German rule.

Whoever gave the order to Breitner to redeploy those companies may not have been aware that the Georgians on Texel had not previously been asked to play a front-line combat role against the Western Allies, unlike other Georgians who had fought in Normandy. The 822nd Battalion's war had so far consisted mainly of defending Hitler's Atlantic Wall, and earlier anti-partisan actions in the east. They had little appetite for going into combat against British and Canadian troops.

Breitner was ordered to lead his Georgians off the island on the morning of Friday 6 April. As the major recalled the events of that day, the order to take his Georgian troops to the mainland was unexpected. He had assumed that he and his men would spend the remaining weeks of the war on the island, waiting for the fighting to end. The Georgian battalion he commanded had earlier been reinforced with German soldiers and transformed into the 177th Infantry Regiment. The order he received specified that most of the regiment was now to head for the front. The others, remaining behind on Texel, would protect the coastline. He passed on the order to the highest-ranking Georgian officer, Shalva Loladze. Loladze was told to instruct his men to be ready to leave the island in the morning.

But instead of going to the front to fight the advancing British and Canadian forces, the Georgians had other plans.

A Meeting in the Woods

Texel is not a heavily forested island, but there are some small groves of trees here and there. The western part of the island contains some dense growths of fir. This is where six Georgian officers decided to meet shortly after Breitner passed on the order to Loladze. It was a meeting that they all knew would eventually happen, and a decision that they would sooner or later have to take.

The first to speak was Evgeni Artemidze, who had earlier made contacts with the local resistance on the island, and before that with Annie Klein and the Dutch Communist Party on the mainland. He made the case for a mutiny right then, that very night. While most people later assumed that the reason for the revolt was to send a message to the Soviets that the Georgians were not traitors – and thereby save their lives when the war ended – Artemidze actually made a somewhat different case on that day.

He argued that when the 300 or so Georgians reached the front they would almost certainly surrender to the Allies at the first opportunity. There was plenty of precedent for this in the Georgian Legion, many of whose soldiers had gone back to the Soviet side when they had the chance. Much more of this was happening as the war was coming to an end. If the men surrendered to the Allies, he said, the Germans would take their revenge on the remaining Georgians on Texel. In order to prevent that from happening, the redeployment to the mainland must be stopped. The others were in agreement, understanding full well what was going to happen. It was time to bring the war to Texel.

Artemidze recalled the discussion long after the war:

> The Germans decided to send half of our battalion to the front and to leave the other half on Texel. And if the Georgians would betray the Germans and join the British they would kill the Georgians on Texel... We decided it was better to die for a common goal: rebel against the Germans. If we died, then so be it. If we survived, we would be seen as loyal to the Soviet Union.[1]

Loladze agreed with him, and is reported to have said, 'It is very fortunate that the Germans have allowed us to keep our weapons and have even given us extra ammunition for the journey. It will be their own downfall.'

The Georgian officers came up with a plan. They decided to form six groups of about 100 men, who were each given key targets to capture and hold. Gongladze was given the task of conquering the towns of De Koog on Texel's North Sea coast and Oudeschild, the harbour facing the Dutch coast. Nozadze was given responsibility for the western part of the De Vlijt airfield and Artemidze was to occupy the eastern part.

The northern artillery battery was the responsibility of Matchaidze and Gujabidze. Melikia was instructed to seize control of the southern battery. The two batteries were under the command of the Germany Navy, and their commander did not trust the Georgians. He had denied them access to the batteries, which were manned by some 250 German soldiers each. The batteries were heavily defended, surrounded by minefields and barbed wire, and the Georgians understood that this would be the most challenging part of their operation.

Loladze, who was in overall command of the rebellion, was to take over the Hotel de Lindeboom, the German headquarters in Den Burg, as well as the nearby battalion headquarters in the bunker complex of Texla, just outside the town.

These were all vitally important targets. The airfield needed to be captured to allow Allied planes to land, once the Allies had been informed that a successful rebellion had taken place. The port at Oudeschild needed to be in Georgian hands to prevent the landing of German reinforcements. The two artillery batteries on the north and south of the island were also essential. If they remained in German hands, the guns could be turned on the island itself, putting the whole project at risk. And the capture of the German headquarters, including Major Breitner, was vital as it would cut off the head of the German forces and prevent a well-organised counter-attack. All this was clear to the Georgian leaders.

The operation was scheduled to begin at 01:00. Most of the Germans would be asleep in their beds. The Georgians would enter the barracks and kill the Germans silently, using their bayonets, razors or daggers to slit their throats. They would avoid firing weapons, which might raise the alarm.

The Dutch resistance were alerted at the last minute to the imminent rebellion. In the early evening of Thursday 5 April, not long after the Georgian rebel leaders finished their meeting in the woods, the brothers Huug and Cor Snoek, who were members of the Dutch underground, had a meeting with Artemidze. They had been in touch with each other for some time. Artemidze told them that just after midnight, the war would come to Texel – and to be prepared.

The Snoek brothers knew that the Georgians had long planned on this possibility, but they had thought it no longer likely to happen, especially with the end of the war now in sight. Jacob Keijzer had expected a revolt on 1 May, which was several weeks away. The Snoeks wanted to spread the word to other members of the resistance, but the German curfew had already come into force. They could not move around the island, and were themselves in hiding. As a result, most of the Dutch people on Texel would find out about the uprising only after it had begun.

The Georgian soldiers themselves were also given very little advance warning. 'An hour before, every Georgian soldier was told which bunker to enter and which German to kill,' said Grisha Baindurashvili. 'We had everything figured out.'[2]

Because the Germans and Georgians would be wearing the same uniforms during the fighting, the rebels came up with a password that they were certain the Germans wouldn't be able to pronounce. They choose a phrase in Russian, and it became the name of their operation: 'Den Rozhdenyi'.

It meant 'day of birth'.

The Revolt Begins

The revolt began in Den Burg with the firing of flares into the pitch-black night – just as the Ukrainians who rebelled against the Waffen-SS in the eastern part of France had done the previous summer. All across Texel, the signal alerted the Georgian soldiers to rise up and kill their German allies and masters. In the course of just a few minutes, they killed over 400 German soldiers. Many were slain in their beds, their throats cut.[3]

But the attempt to do this silently did not go as planned. In some cases they chose to use hand grenades and machine guns.

Valiko Zhgenti remembered leading a Georgian platoon that night. 'I was attacking a bunker which contained four officers,' he said. 'I shot two of them, but then a bullet lodged in my arm. Using my left arm, I stabbed the remaining two like dogs. Enraged by my injury, my platoon and I killed another thirty Germans before advancing to the batteries.'[4]

Dutch resistance fighter Huug Snoek worked with the Georgians in those first hours:

> The skirmishes continued all night. We stopped Germans who were lost and asked for the Georgian code word. None of them knew it. Actually, I couldn't pronounce it either, but we didn't waste time on words. The Georgians were all marksmen and every German we came across was shot. They were all shot in the head, straight through their German helmets.[5]

One of the few Germans who survived that night was Johnny Teuwsen, who was Dutch but had German parents and was therefore compelled to serve in the German Army. 'The revolt took us completely by surprise,' he said, though he knew that the Georgians were about to be redeployed to the front lines:

> That evening, a Georgian delivered us a bottle of vodka. They probably wanted us to sleep well, but I don't like vodka. There were 10 of us in the bunker when all hell broke loose. The guards were shot dead and a hand grenade was thrown into the bunker, injuring my chest and wrist. I wanted to run outside but the others tried to stop me.

He finally managed to get out of the bunker only to find himself standing face-to-face with an armed Georgian soldier:

> I wrestled the gun from his hands and fled into the night. Then I jumped into a canal and stayed there for a couple of hours with my head just above the water. When things quieted down I fled into a barn owned by a farmer I knew.

Teuwsen's behaviour was exactly what the Georgians themselves would be doing in just a few days when the tide of battle turned against them. In Teuwsen's case, he knew many of the farmers and had done some trading with them. 'Being Dutch, they trusted me,' he said. 'I was given civilian clothing and thanks to the farmers, I survived.'[6]

Though not every objective was achieved by the Georgians in those first few hours, most were. Gongladze said: 'In planning the attack, we calculated exactly the number of Germans that had to be killed and by whom. Some had to kill ten, others just five or one.' He recalled quickly completing his mission in De Koog and coming over to Texla to report to Loladze. He was sent on to take over the harbour at Oudeschild. 'The harbour was strongly defended by the Germans but we accomplished the task, using additional artillery, a mortar and a heavy machine gun.'[7]

Breitner Escapes

Major Breitner remembered the uprising as beginning at around midnight. He recalled hearing shots being fired 'everywhere' and seeing the flares.

Breitner got lucky. He was not where the Georgians expected him to be. According to his own account, 'I was troubled by my kidneys all through the war and was receiving treatment on Texel. I often had to go to the toilet and that night I had just walked outside when I saw signal flares and heard gunshots and screaming.'[8] This is not the story told by locals on Texel today. They recall that Breitner had a mistress on the island, and he was spending the night with her, rather than in his own barracks. Local guides will take you to see the woman's house, which is still standing.

The flares were fired off at a time when several hundred of the Georgians were supposed to be withdrawing from their positions to the east coast of the island. This was in preparation for their departure in the morning to the mainland, where they were due to join the battle against advancing Allied forces. Breitner said that he assumed that the noise was being made by Georgians celebrating their departure. He thought they were setting off fireworks. This was the first of many strange things that Major Breitner would say about that evening.

Why would the Georgians be celebrating? 'Considering their mentality, I did not think this out of ordinary,' Breitner later said. But their posting on Texel made them among the luckiest soldiers in the German Army. The island had barely been touched by the war, which – it was clear to all – would be ending in a few weeks at most. Why would they have wanted to go the mainland to engage in actual combat, risking their lives? Or did Breitner really believe that the Georgians were somehow ideologically committed to the German cause and were keen to take part in a futile last battle to defend the Reich? After all, they had all sworn 'to be honest, to work conscientiously, to fulfil all orders received from one's commanders, to love Hitler and to work sincerely for Germany'.

Soon Breitner realised that it was not a celebration. The noises had increased. From a nearby bunker, he heard shots and men shouting. 'It occurred to me,' he later recalled, 'that the Allies might be landing on the island or the Dutch were rising up.' And those were the three possibilities he considered that night: a Georgian celebration, an Allied landing or a Dutch uprising.

A fourth possibility, the idea that his loyal Georgian soldiers, men he had served with for years, men he had taken home with him on leave from the front, would be rising up and killing their fellow Wehrmacht soldiers by slitting their throats as they slept – that idea didn't even make his top three guesses at what was happening. 'I did not even think about the Georgians at that time,' he admitted.

Within minutes of the outbreak of the rebellion, Breitner found himself in the company of two other German officers and ordered them to accompany him to a nearby bunker. He instructed a *Sönderführer*, a civilian expert attached to the Army, to try to raise the alarm by radio.

'Suddenly, my Georgian orderly was right in front of me with a gun and a steel helmet,' remembered Breitner. 'I took his gun away and asked what he thought he was doing. Apparently, he didn't want to kill me, perhaps because I once took him on leave.'[9] Breitner did not tell us what became of that Georgian orderly, now disarmed and facing an enraged German officer; it is believed that he was killed by the rebels.

Breitner and the two other officers were now heading by foot to the Texla bunker complex. 'I let an officer walk in front of me,' Breitner said. 'Suddenly as we approached the bunker, a shot rang out and the man fell down dead. Only then did everything become clear to me.'

Now it was time to change direction, as it had become obvious that Texla had already fallen to the Georgians. Breitner turned away, heading quietly to the southern part of the town. He nearly ran into a Georgian patrol. 'They were shooting Germans on sight,' he said. 'I lay in a field and watched them go about their murderous business for a few hours before I finally managed to slip away to the southern battery.'

The southern battery had not fallen into Georgian hands. It remained a German-held position until the very end of the war. When Breitner reached the battery he learned that while the soldiers there knew that an uprising had taken place, they were unaware of just how serious things had become. From the southern battery, Breitner radioed the German forces in Den Helder, and just a few hours later the first reinforcements began to arrive.

Breitner's report, which has gone down in history as '*Sondermeldung Texel*' ('Special Message Texel'), was forwarded to the *Führerbunker* in Berlin. Hitler had been living there, deep under the Reich Chancellery, since mid-January 1945. By April, he was directing armies which no longer existed to defend an empire that was growing smaller by the hour. Soon Berlin itself would be encircled, with every available

German mobilised to mount a last-ditch defence of the Reich capital.

Hitler was furious when he read Breitner's message, as the Georgians who were busy slaughtering German soldiers on Texel were at the time still wearing the uniforms of the Wehrmacht and had sworn allegiance to him. In the eyes of the Nazi leaders, those Georgians were traitors, deserving of no mercy. The reply from the *Führerbunker* came quickly and instructed the German forces on Texel to 'kill all Georgians immediately'.[10]

It was eventually made clear to the German soldiers sent to carry out this order that the Georgians, if captured, were to be stripped of their German uniforms as they no longer had the right to wear them.

'Something Incredible Had Happened'

Though the local Dutch population on Texel had not been given advance warning of the Georgian uprising, they soon became aware of what was going on. 'On April 6th we were woken up early in the morning by excited neighbours bringing news that the Russians had mutinied,' recalled Hans Verhoeven, a twelve-year-old boy on Texel at the time:

> We had indeed heard gunfire during the night but thought they were on exercise again. But when two Russians walked into the school playground and fired their rifles triumphantly into the air, shouting that all the Germans were '*kaput*', we realised that something incredible had happened.

It was the long-awaited day of liberation, a celebration that was already taking place all across the Netherlands as towns and villages fell to the advancing Allies:

> It appeared that we had suddenly been liberated by the Russians! The new enemies of our enemy had become our friends overnight – at a heavy price as we would find out. The Dutch tricolour appeared outside many houses and people gathered around the school which served as an information centre. Most information consisted of rumours, we soon discovered.[11]

One cannot help be reminded of a similar Dutch reaction during Operation Market Garden a few months earlier when American, British and Polish forces made their bold dash across the Netherlands in an attempt to put an early end to the war. Though they failed to achieve their objective, they were everywhere welcomed as liberators, as the local Dutch population brought out the flags to celebrate with the troops.

On Texel, everyone seemed to be converging on the bunker in Texla, which was now functioning as the rebel headquarters. Eventually the leaders of the Dutch resistance arrived as well. Jacob Keijzer, the deputy commander of the resistance, lived in Den Burg, but had been staying overnight at a flower bulb farm. He rushed over to Texla in the morning.

The leader of the resistance, Wim Kelder was awakened and taken to meet the Georgians:

> When they shot at me, I thought at first that it was an exercise. Texla was in chaos. Artemidze was walking around in a totally agitated state. He said that he had killed 28 Germans. The trenches were full of dead bodies, and more and more civilians were arriving to Texla.'

The Rebellion Spreads

The uprising spread across the island, as the Georgians attempted to seize control of each of the German strongpoints.

They seized control of a bunker complex called Ongeren, thinking that they had killed all twenty-five of the Germans who were there. But it turned out that three of Germans survived, hidden in a ditch. At 08:00, the Georgians left the bunker, all its weapons intact, to head off to battle in the northern part of the island. Later the Germans returned to Ongeren, and were able to use the weapons the Georgians had carelessly left behind.

In De Koog they managed to kill thirty Germans, but did not immediately get control over the town. Germans remained in some of the houses, and continued to control one of the bunkers.

By 07:00, six hours into the rebellion, Georgian soldiers had arrived in Oudeschild. After getting control of an artillery piece they opened fire on the foxholes and the artillery battery in the harbour. By midday the town with its port was in their hands.

At 09:30 in De Koog, the Georgians made another attempt, this time using hand grenades, to wrest control of the bunker, but failed again. The fight against the Germans was turning out to be more difficult than the rebels had imagined at first.

The village of Oosterend in the eastern part of Texel had very few German troops, but there were around half a dozen living in what was called 'the doctor's house'. Those men woke up in the morning and learned what had happened across the island. They panicked and emerged from the house to find many of the villagers waiting outside. The Germans had their guns at the ready, but one of the older locals intervened and calmed them down. They shot no one, and left the village in peace.

There were some Georgians encamped at the lighthouse on the northern tip of the island. This would later become an important location for fighting in the final days of the revolt. On the first night, the rebels managed to cut the throats of most of the Germans there, but a number managed to escape. Some fled to the relative safety of the northern battery, which like the southern one, did not fall into Georgian hands.

In the village of De Cocksdorp, not far from the lighthouse, the Georgians failed to attack an important roadblock, allowing the Germans to flee the following evening. Cornelia Boon-Verberg, who lived in the village, knew the Georgians well, and had been forewarned about their rebellion. They asked her how the Dutch would respond to their uprising, though there was no plan to involve them directly in the fighting. She had a radio and could listen to the BBC. But nothing was being reported about the rebellion on Texel. The rebels did not have access to a working transmitter and were unable to pass on the news of their uprising. But the Allies would find out soon enough, thanks to Bletchley Park, where German radio communications were being monitored and decrypted.

By the end of that first night, an estimated 412 Germans had been killed.

The Dutch Join the Fight

Loladze and the other Georgians realised that though they had taken the initiative, they had little chance of defeating the Germans without support from the Dutch resistance. He met leaders of the Dutch underground who had been summoned to the Texla bunker complex, now serving as the rebel headquarters. He told the resistance leaders that the uprising had broken out across the Netherlands, all the way to Amsterdam, and that on Texel itself all the military strongholds had been taken by the Georgians. The Allies, he said, were on their way. None of this was true, as Loladze almost certainly knew.

He gave some orders to the resistance leaders, demanding for example that members of the fascist NSB be arrested. They agreed to this, but not to the Georgian demand that they be shot. Instead, they were detained in Den Burg's town hall. Some of those NSB leaders would later play helpful roles in restraining the Germans when Dutch lives were on the line.

Slowly the islanders began to learn what had happened overnight. Jan Roeper said:

> By about 9 a.m. we learned more and we heard the attacks in Den Burg. During the morning people arrived who had fled Den Burg to go to the countryside. People we knew came to us. Then they were at Texla. From our house we could see the 60 bunkers surrounding it. We saw that they raised the Dutch flag there. We learned quite quickly that three-quarters of Texel had been liberated.[12]

Another Texelian remembered that 'in the village the flags were raised. We in the *polders* found out a bit later. There wasn't a lot of communication. People from the villages had to tell you what they had heard.'

Dutch and Soviet flags were now hanging from buildings in Den Burg. But this was a premature celebration, as it turned out that there were still a few German soldiers in Den Burg, in the Hotel De Texel and scattered elsewhere throughout the town, and they had fired some shots at the

Georgians. The rebels ordered the Germans in the hotel to surrender, telling them that if they did not do so, the hotel would be blown up. They were promised that if they handed in their weapons, no harm would come to them. Meanwhile, the Dutch civilians who had been in the hotel fled. The Germans in the hotel surrendered and were taken to Texla – where they were shot. Neither side was taking any prisoners.

Loladze issued a proclamation calling on Dutch men to report. A poster was printed and put up around Den Burg. It read:

ORDER

ALL men must report to leader Loladze on Texla. Anyone disobeying will be severely punished.

Texel, 6 April 1945. The deputy commander Texel.[13]

About 200 men showed up, and it turned out that about half of them had some military experience. Weapons were passed out to fifty of them. Addressing them, the Georgian commander declared:

The rebellion against the hated oppressor has started in the whole of Holland. I appreciate it very much that you've come to fight with us as comrades. We have reached the point of no return. Long live Holland. Long live the Soviet Union.[14]

Of course no rebellion had started up 'in the whole of Holland' and Loladze surely knew this even if the Dutch did not. In fact, by the time Loladze delivered his speech, the tide was already starting to turn against the rebels on Texel itself.

Henk de Bloois was among the Dutch men who reported for duty, wearing his old clogs. 'We were given weapons and ordered to collect ten German officers, who had surrendered voluntarily, from Den Burg,' he recalled. 'We did as asked but the prisoners were lined up in front of the bunker and shot through the head by the Georgians.' These may have been the men who surrendered at the Hotel de Texel. He continued: 'I considered that a little too crude, because I wasn't used to it. But we were part of the operation and then you have to go along. Afterwards we received more weapons, hand grenades, carbines, etc. About 20 of us were transported by lorry to Oudeschild.'[15]

'Shortly thereafter, I received a message from our people about a concentration of German troops near Den Hoorn,' remembered Jacob Keijzer. Den Hoorn was near the southern battery:

> I reported this to Loladze, but he said it was impossible as the group led [by] Melikia had been detailed to take the southern battery. He had hardly finished saying this when the first shells exploded on Texla. I remarked sarcastically to Loladze that these shells must also be coming from his men. The situation was very tense and civilians were falling victim to the shells. The Georgian leadership began preparing to leave and I had to decide what should be done about the civilians who had come up to Texla in answer to the summons. One group had already gone to Oudeschild but I sent the rest home.

One of the Dutch men who reported to Texla as Loladze had ordered explained why. 'I felt I had to participate,' he said. 'I'm good with guns . . . In February I learned that my father had been killed in Neuengamme.' Neuengamme was a network of concentration camps in northern Germany. 'So then you want to get even,' he explained.[16]

Another one remembered: 'I went there as well. By myself, I think. I was walking past the cemetery and the first shells from the south battery or Den Helder were already screeching through the air and exploded. I can recall hearing the shell splinters hitting the garden fences. I lay low for a while.'[17]

One islander recalled that 'The Georgians claimed they controlled the whole island. We believed them. But it became clear that the south battery with its four heavy cannons and the north battery weren't under their control. And they hadn't taken the forts with cannons in Den Helder into account.'[18]

Though nearly all the Germans who fell into Georgian hands were killed, some got lucky. One of them was the military chaplain Theo Pieper, who regularly came to the island to organise religious services:

> I always stayed at Hotel De Lindeboom. On the evening of April 5, we were drinking wine and I can still remember my

colleague fleet chaplain Haake saying it is incredible we were stationed on such a peaceful island while the war was so near. Major Breitner was also always optimistic. He said: 'The war is almost over and I can trust my troops.' A few hours later, I was awakened by gunshots. When I looked through the window, someone fired at me. There were dead bodies lying in front of the hotel.[19]

Like Major Breitner, Theo Pieper decided to run off to the safety of the southern battery. He escaped the Hotel De Lindeboom through the back door, but he was stopped by a Georgian and brought back to the rebel headquarters in Texla. 'Suddenly, I realised that my final hour had some,' he said. 'From their commands, I understood that they wanted to execute me. I screamed that I wanted to talk to a Russian officer who could understand German. I wanted to make clear that I was a chaplain. As a result, they locked me in a small bunker.'

It was one of very few examples of mercy shown by either side in the days to come.

War Crime

Within hours of the beginning of the Georgian uprising, the Germans retaliated, choosing a soft target: Dutch civilians. Fourteen men were arrested in Den Burg. They seem to have been chosen at random, picked up on the street, and accused by the Germans of helping the Georgian rebels.

The men were taken in an open truck towards De Mok, on the southern end of the island. En route, four of the men managed to escape by jumping out of the truck. When they reached the beach facing Mok Bay, the Germans shot and killed the remaining ten captives. The victims were Wim and Piet Keijzer, Andries and Herman Pen, Johan Duinker, Kees Witte, Gerrit Broekman, Jan Witte, Jos Oremus, and Piet Ruimers. Their bodies were not found for another six weeks.

This was the first war crime committed by the German forces during the fighting on Texel. By the end, seventy-nine more Dutch civilians had been killed. According to one historian, 'Civilians bore the brunt of German reprisals. Children who had been sent to the island from Amsterdam to recuperate were among the final death toll of eighty-nine civilians.'[20]

Within a few hours of the Soviet and Dutch flags being raised above Texla, the bunker complex had to be evacuated. Loladze's slogan of 'Texel is free, long live the Soviet Union, long live Holland' turned out to have been premature.

The German counter-attack had begun.

Chapter 10

The German Counter-Attack

At first, it all seemed to be going quite well for the Georgians.

About three-quarters of the island was in their hands within a few hours. They had taken both the airfield and the port in Oudeschild, as well as the lighthouse on the northern tip of the island. The main towns, including Den Burg, and the German headquarters in the Texla bunker complex were under their control. Over 400 Germans, officers among them, were dead. The Dutch were lining up to receive their weapons and join in the fight.

The Georgians had not achieved *all* their strategic objectives, to be sure. Critically, the two batteries, on the northern and southern parts of the island, were not taken by the Georgian detachments sent to do so. And Major Breitner, commander of the 822nd Battalion, had escaped – and had sounded the alarm. These failures by the Georgian rebels proved to be fatal. By midday on 6 April, the German counter-attack had begun, and the tide of battle immediately began to turn. The Georgians would never again regain the initiative.

As one Texelian recalled, 'We knew by nine o'clock in the morning we weren't going to win. Texla was under fire by then. Some of the volunteers were dead or wounded. I said to my brother, there are things in store for us that we weren't counting on.'[1]

Even before the Germans landed reinforcements and began their reconquest of the island, they used the tools they had at hand to strike hard at the rebellious Georgians. Foremost among these were the naval batteries on the island, and also nearby ones whose guns could reach Texel. These included the batteries at Den Helder on the mainland, and on Vlieland, the island just north-east of Texel.

Before the shelling began, Major Breitner decided to give the

Georgians an ultimatum. But he had to find a way to deliver the message to them. Knowing that any German soldiers he sent to them would likely be executed, he decided to pick two Georgians who had been stationed on the mainland, in Den Helder. They went to Loladse's headquarters, riding their bicycles and carrying white flags through the streets of Den Burg. Breitner's ultimatum told the Georgians that they had until 15:00 to surrender and hand in their weapons. If they did not do so, the Germans would open an artillery bombardment of the town.

Loladse read the ultimatum – and then tore up the paper. The two Georgians sent to deliver the message then chose to join the Georgian rebels and did not return to the German side.

Loladze ordered a withdrawal of his forces from Den Burg in order to spare the town, but it didn't work – the Germans went ahead with their bombardment. The bombardment was fierce as German guns which were designed to pierce the thick armour of Allied ships were turned against the little villages and farms of Texel. By some accounts, 2,000 artillery rounds were fired that first day. There was considerable damage, with dozens of homes in Den Burg hit, fifty of them destroyed. There were large numbers of casualties, including many civilian deaths.

One eyewitness described the German artillery barrage many years later:

> We were still sitting at the table after dinner and we heard a shot. We heard a few more. My father said 'They're aiming at us'. While he's saying that all hell broke loose ... My father was hit in the head. I think he still looked at us. It was a bloodbath. His head fell to the side. My mother ran to him and grabbed him. It was pandemonium. It was incredible. My mother ran outside. She shouted for help. The Germans sent her back. But then they noticed she was covered in blood. The neighbours came out of their house.[2]

One of the local men recalled:

> Boatloads of Germans were arriving from Den Helder. They started to fight the Georgians. That went one way. The under-

ground resistance was there already. They figured they would liberate the island. But they hadn't counted on the supply of fresh troops.[3]

Fred Simon's Story

One of those fresh troops to arrive that day was Fred Adolf Simon. Simon, who was born in Germany but raised in the United States, wrote a memoir of his experience as a German soldier some sixty years afterwards.[4] He was initially deployed to a Panzergrenadier unit on the Eastern Front and was badly wounded there. He then spent several years doing various jobs far behind the lines. In 1945 he was transferred to Den Helder. Mostly his unit drilled under the command of a First World War veteran, which he hated. But all that came to an end on 6 April 1945.

'We were alerted,' he recalled. 'Off the tip of Den Helder was the first Friesian Island, called Texel. On this small island were SS officers and men training a battalion of Russian soldiers; these were Georgians.' While serving on the Eastern Front, Simon had been one of the German soldiers who came closest to reaching the Soviet Georgian frontier before being forced to retreat. Ironically, the first Georgians he actually encountered were on Texel.

Simon was not a historian, and his memoir reflects what he probably heard from other men. He continued with a somewhat inaccurate account of what was taking place on Texel.

> They [the Georgians] had volunteered just to get out of the prison camps. They were trained to take the place of German soldiers, anti-aircraft gunners, truck drivers, etc. So the German soldiers could be sent to the front. But things went wrong. During the night from the sixth to the seventh of April, these Russian soldiers, wearing German uniforms, killed all the German personnel except the commander.

That was largely true, and the next sentence reflects one of the rumours that circulated among both the Dutch civilians and the German soldiers: 'We learned later that he [Major Breitner] had been on the mainland visiting his girlfriend.'

Simon wanted to emphasise that the men at the disposal of the German Army to deal with the uprising on Texel were not the crack troops that later historians would make them out to be:

> One of my other duties was to train new arrivals, seventeen- and eighteen-year-olds, just drafted. I was old, twenty-two, an old hand with front-line experience on the Russian front. I had to train them on an old 37-mm anti-tank gun. We had only anti-tank ammunition.

On the morning of the Georgian mutiny, Simon's commander was ordered to take his men to Texel. 'Our commander scraped together a group of guys from near and far,' Simon wrote. 'Now, most of us were previously wounded soldiers, not fit for front-line duty, plus some old guys, aged forty and even fifty. My gun crew was made up of eighteen-year-olds. What a fighting force!'

To emphasise how unprepared they were to take on the Georgians on Texel, Simon referred to his men as 'this bunch' who were 'to be ferried over to the islands – about 200 strong, against about 1,500.' This was, of course, an exaggeration – there was nothing like that number of Georgians on the island. But this is no doubt what the German soldiers were told. 'Most of the Russians', he heard, ' were on the northern end of the island where the harbour was located.'

After being ferried over to Texel, Simon wrote, 'We pushed slowly forward towards Den Burg. We were fired on from the church steeple. I was ordered to fire one shell into the steeple; it must have hit the bell it clanged so frightfully. The poor guy up there must have gone nuts.'

They kept moving through Den Burg until they came to a compound, presumably the bunker complex at Texla which had been the German battalion's command post and later the headquarters of the rebels:

> We found all of the German soldiers killed, their throats slit. I was getting my gun in position. Several shots rang out hitting our shield and bouncing off. One more shot, and of two of my gun crew yelled; one shot had hit both of them, one in the arm, and then it passed right through and hit the other in the leg.

The Georgians had clearly not yet completed their withdrawal from Den Burg at this point.

> I was sitting behind the shield with only my helmet showing [remembered Simon]. But where the muzzle sticks through the shield is a small opening, used to raise and lower the barrel. The next shot hit right in there. The bullet split into several pieces, one hitting me in the forehead and many small splatters all over my face.

It was the second time in the war that Simon had been injured by Red Army fire – though this time the Soviet soldiers were wearing the same uniform that he was.

'Everybody called for a medic,' he wrote:

> He came racing up on a motorcycle with sidecar. We were now sitting behind a hedgerow, but the part he had to drive through on the open road was fully visible to the snipers. Nevertheless, he made it to us without being hit. Going back was a different story, with three wounded and only three seats available on the motorcycle. Oh yes, the way the medic bandaged me, a whole bandage around my head, I could not see a thing.

Thus blindfolded, Simon realised that two other soldiers had squeezed into the sidecar, while he was seated behind the driver. He realised that his body was now between the driver and any Georgian snipers wanting to take a shot. 'Lucky for him, that way he could not be hit, but what about me?' he thought. 'Well he revved up the motorcycle and off we went at breakneck speed, bullets whistling around my head, but nobody got hit.' He was ferried back to the mainland, to the hospital at Den Helder which would soon be full of many other wounded German soldiers.

The battle to take back Texel had just begun.

The Germans Advance

By the end of the first day of fighting, Texel's main town, Den Burg, and the port of Oudeschild were back in German hands. The Georgians still held the airfield and the lighthouse at the island's northern tip, and the village of De Waal, just north-east of Den Burg.

After taking Den Burg, the Germans had moved on to Texla, as Simon remembered. The Georgians had already cleared out, as had the Dutch, fearing reprisals. The Georgian retreat was carried out under the cover of darkness, as the men moved from farm to farm.

The fighting was ferocious from the start, as Breitner recalled:

> We were very angry. Everybody was furious about the way in which the rebels had killed our men. Many people, including naval personnel who weren't trained for land-based combat, volunteered to fight. Any Georgians, who surrendered or were captured, were executed according to martial law.[5]

Breitner tried to explain why the battle to re-take Texel proved so difficult at first. 'The re-conquest of the island proceeded slowly but surely,' he said years later:

> We suffered huge losses because the Georgians resisted fiercely from their entrenched positions around our former strongholds. They had considerable amounts of ammunition. The Georgians were well trained and knew the terrain well. Moreover, they knew they would be killed if caught. Initially we had only light weapons but we continued fighting and even reserve officers, who had experienced the First World War, participated. Everyone realised that we were about to lose the war, but we wanted to take revenge on the Georgians first.

Two companies of Germans had landed east of Oosterend, on the north-eastern side of the island. These troops captured that town and also the village of De Waal. After that, they tried to re-take both the port of Oudeschild and the airfield. The port fell into their hands but the Georgians stubbornly held on to the airfield. These were obviously key strategic targets, especially if the Germans wanted to land more forces – and also to prevent a possible allied landing by air.

A few of the wounded Georgians had been left behind in the bunkers of Texla, in the care of a Dutch doctor and nurse. Shells fell near them, but the doctor and nurse remained at their posts. As Dr Veening recalled:

> Initially, we treated six badly injured Georgians but the Germans dragged them outside and shot them immediately. After the incident, the Georgian casualties were hidden and treated by their own medics. The Georgians were well trained and well fed. I visited some of them in barns and other secret locations. Generally, they recovered quickly.

After this, the Dutch could no longer provide medical care for wounded Georgian rebels, though many did help by offering the rebels food and places to hide – at great personal risk to themselves. The underground movement also supplied the rebels with useful information on German troop movements.

The wounded Germans were taken to hospital in Den Helder, on the mainland, where they joined Fred Simon. Crew members of the ferry *De Voorwaarts* told Huug Snoek that the ship's decks were full of 'many hundreds' of badly injured Germans.[6]

The Dutch civilians, many of whom had reported for duty as Loladze had ordered, decided to leave the rest of the fighting to the Georgians. They knew that if captured by the Germans, they faced certain death. That first day, some of them crawled from barn to barn, looking for safe places on the island to hide.

Piet Vlaming was one of the Dutch men armed and sent by Loladze to Oudeschild to support the Georgians at that strategic port. As the German counter-attack grew in strength, Vlaming went into hiding, but was caught by the Germans. They transported him to Den Burg, where he denied having helped the Georgians. The Germans couldn't prove otherwise, but decided to take him, as they had done earlier with fourteen Dutch men, to De Mok where he would be shot. But at the last minute, the Germans decided they needed the truck for another purpose and his life was saved – and strangely, with the help of local Dutch Nazi, a member of the NSB fascist party.

As he remembered that day, Vlaming said:

> The Germans put me and two of my friends against the wall of Hotel De Lindeboom. They were about to shoot us when the local NSB teacher Goedhart came and interrupted them. He went [to] the German commander to convince him not to kill us. Later they brought us outside a second time, but Goedhart interfered again, and the summary execution was cancelled. Funnily, I wasn't scared anymore. The Germans had beat me so badly, I felt like letting them get on with shooting me.

If the Georgians had had their way, Goedhart and the other NSB members would have been shot. Vlaming's life was saved because the Dutch resistance leaders insisted on detaining, but not shooting, the local fascists. The NSB members who had been held in Den Burg's town hall were sent home. But they remained inactive for the rest of the war.

By the second day of the rebellion, Georgian troops had retreated to De Koog, a town on the western coast of Texel. Orders were given to hold Oosterend, de Waal and the airfield.

As Gongladze, whose unit had captured De Koog and Oudeschild in the initial fighting, recalled: 'We also had to guard the connecting roads to prevent German reinforcements being sent north. We suffered a lot of casualties, but German losses were much higher, because they were attacking while we remained in our strong defensive positions.'

His memory was in accord with Breitner's. This would prove to be a difficult fight for the Germans. Just how difficult can be illustrated by a story Piet Vlaming told. After being spared from execution in Den Burg on the first day of the fighting, he was ordered to assist in the burial of Germans who had died in the battle.

> There was a pile of about [a] hundred German bodies. We had to undress them, take off their boots and their rings, and put all their personal belongings in Red Cross bags. We covered the corpses in paper before burying them. Eventually, we ran out of paper and buried them as they were. The dead bodies in the first pile, victims apparently of the first night, were severely mutilated. Initially, I was almost overcome by the gruesome

work and it took three days before I could taste food again. After that ... well, I suppose you can get used to anything.

... a constant stream of German fatalities arrived at the cemetery in carts confiscated from farmers. We buried at least 600 people within the space of fourteen days. The majority had been shot through the head. The German police commander came by each day, cursing and beating and threatening to kill members of the burial detail.

The Dutch men involved in burying the Germans had had enough of the brutality of this German commander and they passed on the information to the underground. As Vlaming remembered, 'The commander's body arrived the next day for burial.'

It was a very cruel battle from the first day on, with neither side showing any mercy to the other. The Georgians under Loladze's command soon realised that they would have to use the methods of the partisans, and to avoid a direct fight with the stronger German forces. They began using the tactics practised by the very partisans they had fought against on the Eastern Front. And they stubbornly defended the airfield, because they continued to hope that at some point, they would receive help from the Allies.

The Germans took many casualties as they tried to storm the bunkers that surrounded the airfield. The Georgians were no longer in those bunkers but instead waiting nearby in ambush for the German assault. When the Germans moved on the bunkers, they were cut to pieces by Georgian fire from unexpected directions.

Meanwhile, the number of German troops on the island was steadily increasing and their weaponry now began to include heavier armaments.

When the Germans captured Georgians alive, they ordered them to undress, as it was felt that they were unworthy to wear the German uniform. The naked Georgian prisoners were then forced to dig their own graves, and were shot. Some of the naked Georgians managed to flee, hunted by the Germans.

Matchaidze's Georgians had proven unable to capture the northern battery. This failure allowed the Germans to use both the northern and southern guns to support the advance of their reinforcements as they began the reconquest of Texel. The northern battery bombarded the neighbouring village of De Cocksdorp, which had been abandoned by most of the inhabitants. Den Burg received the same treatment. After the bombardment and the Georgian retreat, it seemed for a moment that there would be a rebel counter-attack, as happened at De Waal. Most civilians did not wait around to find out. The Germans did not show any mercy to civilians and shot suspects on the spot.

Events proved that Loladze and Artemidze had been too optimistic when planning the revolt. The rebellion had not spread to the other Eastern Legion battalions camped in the rest of the Netherlands. Once the tide of battle had turned against the Georgians, the uprising on Texel increasingly became a war of attrition. The Georgians were being hunted, and the Germans were doing the hunting. The crucial question was whether the British knew what was happening on Texel and whether they would send help.

When the German counter-attack started and the broadcasting station could not make contact with Britain. Resistance leader Wim Kelder proposed an old plan: sending a boat to England to summon aid.

The Lifeboat

Texel had a lifeboat, the *Joan Hodshon*, which was based near the lighthouse in the village of De Cocksdorp, not far from the battery which remained in German hands.

It was clear from the very beginning that the uprising would fail unless help was obtained from the Allies. As British and Canadian forces were already racing through the Netherlands on their way to the German frontier, and with the fall of Berlin only a month away, it was not unreasonable for the Georgian leaders on Texel to assume that if they could only get the word out, the Allies would come to their rescue. But with no access to a radio transmitter, the rebels needed to send men across the North Sea to deliver a message personally to London.

The Georgians worked with Kelder and together they decided to make the attempt on the night of 8 April. But all did not go according to plan. The boat sat on rails which were used to put it out to sea – but these had become covered with sand. A ferryman called Jan Bakker went over to De Cocksdorp to find volunteers to help him move the boat. Four men who had been hiding in a cellar came out to help. One of those, Klaas Doornekamp, made the case that he should be allowed on the boat as a reward for helping out.

Others recruited by the resistance for the journey included First Mate Klaas van der Kooij, who proved to be essential in navigating the ship towards its goal. His cousin also came on board and they smuggled out other Dutch civilians who had been in hiding along with them. Other members of the crew included Wim de Bloois, Remmert Hooijberg, Cor Dros, Marinus Kooger, Jaap Knol, and Jaap Westdorp. Four Georgians came along too. They carried their weapons with them.

Years later Jan Bakker remembered the night they set off:

> In terms of the weather, the night was perfect. But our fate would have been sealed had the Germans seen us as we pushed off from the coast. Fortunately, they were more concerned about the Georgians on land than looking out to sea. Later we heard that our departure could be heard all the way into the village. So we were very lucky. We were moving in the direction of the northern battery. Once we reached open sea, we steered north-west to escape from the island.[7]

Marinus Kooger remembered some tension between the Dutch and their Georgian passengers:

> The journey went well and we didn't come across any Germans. We had asked the Georgians to get rid of their weapons but they refused. We wanted to claim that we had fled the violence if the Germans stopped us. Having guns on board would have ruined the story. After a while, the Georgians became terribly seasick and were dead to the world, so we took the opportunity to throw their weapons overboard.[8]

As Evgeni Artemidze later recalled, 'We sent a delegation of eight people to England. Four Dutch and four Georgians. But we lost contact. We never heard from them.'[9]

After twenty-four hours at sea, they approached the Norfolk coast, and van der Kooij fired off a flare to attract attention. An RAF reconnaissance plane spotted it, and guided them to the coast. They landed on the beach at Mundesley, where they were greeted by the Home Guard. The Guardsmen were startled to see four men in German uniforms among the Dutch civilians.

The Georgians were not welcomed as heroes. As was the case with any Soviet citizens captured while serving on the German side, they were whisked off to Kempton Park, in Sunbury on Thames. Their interrogation there on 11 April, the record of which is held by the National Archives in Kew, provides us with the first real-time, eyewitness account of the uprising as seen by the Georgian side.

In a top secret report, the four Georgians were named as David Gavashvili, Simon Karkashadze, Akaki Matchaidze and Georgi Reviashvili. The report, which is rich in useful intelligence for the Allies, was distributed widely by MI19, a branch of British Military Intelligence, with over sixty copies in circulation, including to the Supreme Headquarters of Allied Forces in Europe.[10]

The interrogators were able to sum up the story of the rebellion in a single paragraph before explaining how they came to be in England:

> On 5 Apr 45 the Georg Inf Btl 822 consisting mainly of Georgians and stationed on the Dutch island of Texel revolted against the German Offrs, NCOs and men. The Germans, approx. 400 in number, were soon disposed of and the Russians, now under comd of their own Offr. Lt. (former Capt. of the Red Army) Loladse proceeded with mopping up operations in which they were greatly assisted by the local Dutch population.
>
> ... The above four PW who arrived in a motor launch in the early hours of 10 Apr 45 at Mundesley, Norfolk together with ten Dutch civilians were sent to England for help against German resistance which could not be overcome by the insufficiently armed Russians. They were instructed to ask primarily for RAF action against the German artillery. They left De Cocksdorp

on 8 Apr 45 at 2359 hrs and this Report covers the events up to that time.[11]

The rest of the report went into considerable detail about the uprising. It reported first of all on the parts of Texel believed to be held by the Georgian rebels. There were five of these – the lighthouse, the village of De Cocksdorp, the airfield, the area around De Koog and the dunes dominating the west coast of the island, and the port town of Oudeschild on the eastern side of the island. By this point, very early in the rebellion, the Georgians had already lost control of the largest town, Den Burg.

The Georgians were asked to describe the 'points of local German resistance', which they did in considerable detail. There were two of these worth highlighting. One was the northern battery, which consisted of two 7.5 cm guns, one 8.8 cm flak gun, one 8.1 cm mortar and three coastal defence guns (calibre unknown) which according to the Georgians were pointing west 'with limited traverse'. The southern battery was also reported to remain in German hands, and had two 15.2 cm French guns and one or two 2 cm flak guns.

The Georgians seemed unaware that the German artillery may have been firing on the island, assuming that their guns were trained on the sea. They told their British interrogators about the shelling which had taken place on the first day of the rebellion. As they put it, the two German batteries had working radios and used these to direct artillery fire from the island of Vlieland, just north of Texel.

The British interrogators were told about the German decision to launch a counter-offensive, describing the forces that arrived on Texel after news of the rebellion reached Berlin. On the first day, according to the Georgians, about two platoons of German marines landed at Oudeschild, but 'they were routed' by the rebels.

Two days later, another two companies of Germans landed east of Oosterend, north of Oudeschild. Those Germans had greater success, capturing Oosterend and De Waal. Their objectives after that seemed to be the strategically important airfield, and the port of Oudeschild. These would be essential to land more German troops – and in the case of the airfield, to prevent any Allied help from arriving.

When the four Georgians left the island on the lifeboat, they knew that Loladze 'planned to counter attack the Germans, but the result of this operation is not known'. When asked about the strength of the rebel forces, the Georgians explained that they had about 800 men with the following weapons at hand: sixteen heavy machine guns, eighteen light machine guns, six 8.1 cm mortars, nine 4.5 cm mortars, one 'revolving armoured turret' with a light anti-tank gun in the lighthouse and two 4.5 cm Russian anti-tank guns. They could not give precise details of how much ammunition, food and medical supplies were available, but these were 'considered sufficient to hold out for the time being'. Unfortunately for them, the 'time being' turned out to be another six weeks.

The group on the lifeboat had done as they were told. They gave valuable intelligence to the British interrogators and made it clear exactly what help they needed in order to defeat the German counter-attack then taking place on the island. But aiding the rebellious Georgians did not fit in with Allied plans.

All that seems to have happened as a result of the lifeboat's journey was that the British sent a reconnaissance plane to Texel to monitor what was going on.

The Georgians on Texel were on their own.

Chapter 11

Hunters and Hunted

The battle for Texel raged for several days during which the Germans managed to drive the Georgians out of their strongholds, sending most of them into hiding. A war of attrition then began which lasted until the end of the Second World War in Europe – and beyond.

On 8 April, as the lifeboat prepared to leave on its mission to England, the Germans ordered the islanders to report the presence of any Georgians hiding in or near their homes. Some 3,600 German troops landed on the island, and it appears that they were mostly from the SS. On the following day, the shelling of the island resumed. Two days later, the local Dutch people were able to bury thirty victims and the German artillery went silent. The German commander came to pay his respects to the dead – who had been killed by his side. After the funeral, the shelling resumed and continued for another week.

Partisan Warfare

The Georgians must have learned something from their experience combatting partisans on the Eastern Front. During the weeks of fighting that followed their uprising, despite the upper hand the Germans held in men and equipment, the Georgians made the reconquest of Texel as difficult as they could.

As one Dutch civilian remembered it,

> Later on, the Russians withdrew among the fir trees. They were driven out of the countryside. So then they were in the woods. The Germans didn't really dare to go in there. The Russians could see the Germans coming. The Germans couldn't be sure where they were. When they came close they were shot.[1]

The Georgians relied on the Dutch to hide them from the Germans. One of those who benefited from the Dutch willingness to risk their lives in this way was Evgeni Artemidze himself. A Dutch woman told this story:

> One day they said: 'I'm bringing someone here tomorrow.' That person had to stay with us, because he was important. When that person was brought it turned out to be Artemidze ... My father said: 'What am I going to do with that guy?' We had already slaughtered the pig and put it in preserving jars. There was a small cubicle in a hay clamp. The pig had lived there.
>
> That was where they took Artemidze – to where the family pig had lived. Then her father shaved off Artemidze's black hair. 'With a cap on,' she said, 'he didn't look all that Russian anymore.'[2]

Artemidze had been known to the Dutch as 'Little Stalin'. According to his daughter, this was due to his leadership skills and charisma. But it may also have been due to the fact that he was a Georgian with a bushy moustache.

The Dutch also provided the Georgians with food throughout the uprising. One Texelian remembered how

> A few days later, a German cannon was standing in our farmyard. Right in front of my parents' bedroom window. Some guy was walking around the farmhouse all night to guard that cannon. Despite the guard, the Russians came in their socks, knocked on the window and asked for food. The food was standing ready for them, because they came every day.

Another Dutch civilian recalled:

> Because we helped them out, they didn't go hungry in the woods. It was worse when the German forces searched through the woods. They showed no mercy. The Georgians who were discovered were killed on the spot. They had their skulls bashed in and sometimes their eyes gouged out. Monstrous.[3]

'It Looks Like a Naked Man'

After the Germans began their counter-attack, the Georgians became increasingly dependent on help from the local Texelians – for example, the Eelman family who lived on a farm outside De Koog. As Mrs Eelman remembered, 'My husband was outside with the sheep when bullets suddenly whizzed around his ears. He ran inside and I saw someone in the farmyard. I said: "It looks like a naked man." My husband opened the bedroom window and there he was, a small man without clothes.'

Mr Eelman continued with the story:

> [The Germans] found him and his comrade hiding under reeds in the *polder*. The Georgians were forced to undress themselves and dig their own graves at the side of the road. One of the Georgians was shot dead but the other took a chance and ran. He was very agitated and out of breath when he came to the farm. He had already walked around the farm a few times, trying to decide whether to risk approaching us. We gave him a jacket and he left, knowing the pursuing Germans were probably not far behind.[4]

The Georgian soldier returned a few days later wearing a uniform. The Eelmans learned that his name was Carlos. Their farm became known to the Georgians as a place were they could always find food.

The Eelmans survived the war, but many Dutch civilians who helped the Georgians did not. As one Dutch woman told interviewers many years later, 'Papers were stuck to the trees and they said that if you knew any Russians, you had to report them. Failure to comply meant capital punishment.'

Another Texelian remembered one case in particular, the story of Melle Zegel:

> He lived in Oudeschild. He had taken in a heavily wounded Russian. His wife had bandaged him with sheets. That Russian said: 'I'm dying anyway; go warn the Germans or you and your wife will be killed and your house set on fire.' So he went to Den Burg. Those Germans pulled a dirty trick. They wanted to set an

example. So they detained him. And held a manhunt. And they found the Georgian, of course.

They told him: 'Sorry, we found him before you reported him.' His wife quickly gave their child to the neighbours. His wife and he were executed behind Texla. That was a dirty trick. They wanted to set his house on fire, but it was a row house. The other occupants protested, so they didn't do it. My God. Melle Zegel. Such a dirty trick.[5]

'There Are No Russian Partisans Here!'

One of the last surviving Texel Georgians, Grisha Baindurashvili, gave an interview seventy years after the uprising in which he recalled the period following the German counter-attack:

> We knew that all of us were going to die there. No one would escape alive. We knew that. We fought day and night until the last drop of blood was spilled. There were so many, we couldn't stop them.
>
> Those of us who managed to evade the initial onslaught were hounded at every step, and buildings were torched at the slightest suspicion of anyone hiding inside.
>
> One night, I and two other Georgians were out on a scouting run, to determine if we could get through to our battalion. Suddenly, we heard dogs barking; this meant that a raid was under way. We had no choice but to burrow inside a nearby haystack.

He told a documentary film-maker that some 200 Germans took part in this raid. 'They checked everything: the house, the shed, the stable.'[6]

> The dogs quickly led the Germans to us and were running around the haystack, barking. One of the soldiers brought a ladder and climbed on top of the haystack. If I could draw, I'd draw his face, which I remember perfectly even after 70 years. He was a young man, with black hair. I had a gun trained on him, while his own was in a sling. We spent several seconds

looking straight at each other and then he suddenly turned and left, climbing back down.

Baindurashvili's life had been spared.

> I heard him say 'There are no Russian partisans here!' He said this louder than was necessary, probably so that we could hear as well. I breathed with relief, but kept wondering if this was all just a trick so that they could set the haystack on fire and smoke us out, but nothing of the sort happened.
>
> I spent a lot of time looking for the man who granted me life, but to no avail. I haven't lost hope of finding him yet, no matter how naïve this sounds. I even talked to Dutch journalists a few times, asking them to get the word out.[7]

Battles for the Airfield and Lighthouse

Gongladze was in command of the Georgian rebels defending the Eierland, in the northern part of Texel. Nearly two weeks into the fighting he remained convinced that the Germans could not win due to the Georgians' effective use of guerrilla warfare.

'The Germans used five tanks to try to split the territory and seize the airport,' he said. 'But we replied with antitank rockets and put three tanks out of action. The remaining two tanks fled. The battle for the airport lasted two weeks. On April 17, the Germans captured our strongholds.' The Georgians had suffered many losses in that fight, and Gongladze himself was injured in his leg.[8]

In that combat, as in so many others, the Georgians were aided by local people. The Germans discovered this and pressed local residents to give the names of those who had helped the rebels. One person informed, and three Texelians were arrested and later executed by firing squad in the Erfprins fortress in Den Helder.

Two weeks after the uprising began, with the airfield having fallen to German forces on 17 April, the lighthouse at the northern tip of Texel seemed destined to be the place where the Georgians would make their last stand. It was a heavily fortified position, surrounded by bunkers and minefields. As the Georgians who made the journey to England on the lifeboat told their British interrogators, the lighthouse position included a revolving armoured turret with a light anti-tank gun, as well as other weapons.

Many years later, Grisha Baindurashvili recalled that he was the leader of the first company of Georgians. 'We were in position near the lighthouse. Behind us was the sea. There was nowhere left to go. We had reached the end of the island.'[9]

Major Breitner described the difficulty of removing the Georgians from the lighthouse. 'We could not get them out of there, because we did not have the appropriate weapons,' he recalled. 'The guns of sea and land coastal batteries were directed towards the sea, firmly embedded in the designs of their bunkers and could only target sea targets,' he claimed – though the evidence to the contrary is overwhelming, as it was precisely those batteries which reportedly pounded Den Burg and other parts of Texel in the first days of the fighting, backed up by artillery on the neighbouring island of Vlieland and from Den Helder on the mainland.

It was now 20 April, Adolf Hitler's birthday. 'To take the lighthouse the engineer platoon of the division "Hermann Göring" ... came to the island,' recalled Breitner:

> Under the cover of fire from guns and machine guns, sappers stormed the entrance of the lighthouse, laying a powerful explosive there and filling up the entrance with sandbags. In the explosion, without having the opportunity to deviate, the shock wave went into the tower, causing great destruction. As a result, the Georgians in the tower were destroyed.[10]

Grisha Baindurashvili was one of the few survivors from the lighthouse. He remembered the German assault many years later, including the bombardment from Vlieland, the neighbouring island. 'The lighthouse collapsed,' he said. 'Then they aimed a flame-thrower at us. The whole place around us was on fire. And it was burning us. Out of 120 people only eight survived. The rest were killed by fire. It was one or two in the morning. We managed to escape without being hit by bullets.'[11]

At this point, the fighting on Texel was essentially over.

Beverwijk

While the much-promised uprising of *Osttruppen* across the Netherlands never took place, that doesn't mean that there were no acts of rebellion or sabotage among other Georgian troops serving in the Wehrmacht at that time.

For example, on 20 April, the same day the Germans recaptured the lighthouse on Texel, a group of Georgian soldiers in Beverwijk, north of Zandvoort, were shot by the Germans for having stolen eighty-eight hand grenades. By this point, they would almost certainly have been aware of the events on Texel, and possibly the theft of the hand grenades was part of an attempt to stage their own rebellion.

Some of the bodies of those Georgians buried by the Germans remained without identification until 2019, when the Dutch Forensic Institute was finally able to do a DNA match proving the identity of two of the Georgians now buried in Leusden, south-east of Amsterdam. They were named as Pido Choliashvili and Anton Gviniashvili.[12]

Death of Loladze

For most of the period following the landing of reinforcements on Texel, the German troops were engaged in a mopping-up operation. There were hundreds of Georgians now hiding across the island, and the Germans focussed their attention on killing the Georgian leader, Shalva Loladze. As the Georgians were hiding in barns, in woods, and in ditches, some of their locations were known to local farmers. Most of these provided no assistance at all to the Germans in their search for the rebels. But some did.

One Texel native told the story of how in his own family, which hid two Georgians on their farm, their grandfather took the decision to inform the Germans. He told the Georgians he intended do this, giving them a fifteen-minute warning. But the Georgians did not heed the warning, and when the Germans arrived they were shot and killed. The farmer later admitted to regretting this, and that it was a stain on his conscience his whole life.[13]

Shortly after the capture of the lighthouse, Loladze and a number of his men were hiding on a farm called Plassendaal, near Ruigedijk in the western part of the island. The Germans suspected there were Georgians hiding there, but why they did so is unknown. We do know that the Germans were unaware at the time that Loladze was among them. Some Georgians today have suspicions that Loladze may have had rivals within his own group who betrayed his location to the Germans.

The Germans encircled the farmhouse. Then they set it ablaze, hoping to drive the Georgians out into the open. Those who dashed outside to avoid being burned alive were immediately shot. Some escaped to a nearby pig shed, taking up defensive positions there. But that too was set on fire by the Germans.

Loladze and one other man, reported to be his warrant officer, took shelter in the farm's cellar. After some time, the building had been reduced to a smouldering ruin. When night fell, Loladze and his comrade made a break for it. They hid themselves in a deep ditch nearby. The following morning, a local farmer noticed the two Georgians in the ditch, fast asleep. He told the Germans where they could be found. Locals on Texel say that the identity of the informer was known to the islanders. A heavily armed German patrol arrived on the scene, shooting both the Georgians immediately. They then forced the owner of the farm to bury the bodies.

The German soldiers had no idea who they had just killed. Whatever intelligence they had about the farm did not include the fact that the Georgian commander was one of the people hiding there. As far as they knew, they had managed to kill about ten more Georgians, but they did not know who they were. Three days later, the island's German commander put out a notice to the local population demanding that they report the sightings of any Georgians. The notice specifically mentioned Loladze, who the Germans believed was still alive.

Just a week later, the war would be over in the Netherlands, with the German surrender on 5 May.

Cornelia Boon-Verberg said that she:

> continued to help as long as I could. Georgians were hiding on several farms and we brought them bread. Sometimes they were lying in a haystack and weren't found by the Germans. Then the

Germans would come back with reinforcements and kill the Georgians. Farms were ablaze everywhere.

The help provided by ordinary Dutch civilians was essential to the Georgians' survival. 'Many Georgians survived thanks to the courage of the local people,' Boon-Verberg recalled years later. 'A large number of Georgians hid in Oosterend in particular. Several locals risked their lives by hiding a Georgian because they knew that to help . . . carried the death penalty.'[14]

A Child Remembers

Hans Verhoeven remembered well the aftermath of the Georgian uprising. 'The fighting moved further north so we started to think of a possible return to the school and our house near the airfield.' These had been taken by the Georgians at first, but were recaptured by the advancing German forces.

> Before we could move the Germans began a large scale manhunt to mop up the remaining Russians who, they suspected quite rightly, were hiding among the island population. On April 22nd, 1945, another gruesome and bloody day, they 'trawled' the Eierland *polder* in a broad sweep with soldiers walking side by side ten metres apart. We saw them coming from afar, slowly and menacingly. As they approached across the flat countryside we saw houses, farms and barns going up in flames or being destroyed with grenades. Flames and columns of smoke rose into the sky; the *polder* burned once more.[15]

From time to time, his Uncle Jan walked out of their house to check on the Germans' slow but steady progress.

The mood inside the house, he recalled,

> . . . was very tense. The children sat on the floor at the adults' feet asking anxious questions such as: 'They won't do anything to us, will they? We haven't got any Russians here?' They were not answered. Was this because the adults knew something we didn't? Earlier in the day I had heard Uncle Jan say: 'That hole

is clearly visible now...' referring – so it transpired – to a badly camouflaged dugout he had discovered earlier not far from the house. And indeed, the Germans threw hand grenades into the opening of this hiding place when they found it, although by then it was deserted. Had it sheltered Russians who fled when the Germans approached?

They heard a lot of shooting and people shouting in German:

> I looked out of the front window and saw a man, dressed only in his underwear, run past the chain of soldiers which stretched out from the front of the house to the main road across the fields. Two or three others followed and they were all kicked or beaten. They were Russians who had been flushed out. The Germans told them to discard their uniforms before they were passed along the line, presumably to make them more recognisable and also – it was suggested later – because they considered the mutineers unworthy of wearing German uniforms.

It was a story that repeated itself as the Germans hunted down men who until only recently had been their comrades in arms.

They heard more shooting and shouting, and again Verhoeven looked out the window:

> I saw a man, half undressed, surrounded by a group of soldiers. I remember that he had a black shawl or cloth wrapped around his head. The Germans were beating him with their rifle butts. Suddenly he ducked and disappeared from their midst in a desperate attempt to escape. There was a short burst of rifle fire and then everything went quiet.

The Georgian had been killed. 'His body had been thrown into a well,' Verhoeven wrote.

> After recovering his remains they buried him in a shallow grave beside the track. Many years later, in 1969, I was still able to find the exact spot, a slight hollow in the field from where his body had subsequently been removed to the Russian cemetery.

The German soldiers who were hunting down Georgians were in a 'murderous mood', he remembered:

> They kicked doors open and looked everywhere for more Russians. We were herded into the small living room and a young officer demanded the adults' identity cards. Grandma Stark looked defiantly straight back at the shouting German – I believe he was an SS-officer. He threatened to slap her face because she didn't look at him from the same angle as the photograph on her identity document. Someone held Mr Stark back. Fear welled up in my chest; we were obviously in deep trouble.

The adults, who spoke fluent German, admitted that they had hidden Georgian rebels, but pleaded mitigating circumstances, arguing that the 'Germans themselves had pushed the Russians ahead of them during their manhunt until they had been forced out into the open just near our house. "*Wir haben's nicht gewuss*", was the repeated reply she gave. "We didn't know."' The German officer accepted their explanation, for now, but said he'd be back. Fortunately, he never returned.

'Other people had been summarily executed after Russians were found on their properties,' Verhoeven added. 'I realised how lightly we had escaped.'

As the rebellion came slowly to a close at the end of April, Verhoeven and his family decided to risk going back to their home to see what remained after the fierce fighting.

'We walked past the terrible evidence of heavy fighting along the Post Road and around the airfield,' he wrote:

> We also visited nearby farms to see who was still there. At the once magnificent farm 'Padang' I saw the farmer drag the blackened bodies of his cows from the burnt-out ruin of his cow shed. The carcasses with their sickening smell were pulled onto a large tarpaulin and dragged to a mass grave. In the courtyard of farmhouse 'Gend' I saw a broken and abandoned German artillery piece. Chicken feathers covered everything, including

part of the gun. Something big had exploded here. Maybe there had been a misfire?

They eventually reached the school and their house next door. To their relief, they discovered that the school seemed in good condition. But it 'was filled with bloodied straw and littered with used, blood-drenched bandages. It had been used as a field hospital and was an awful sight.'

As for their house,

> [It was] quite badly damaged externally with many windows shattered and with bullet holes and ragged shrapnel craters everywhere. The interior of the house was in a terrible mess, unbelievably so! Crockery, cutlery, furniture – much of which was not ours – was spread all over the place. The house had served many Germans as a canteen and had been equipped with stuff brought in from neighbouring properties.

They saw Dutch civilians working under German orders carrying uniformed corpses and piling them into a horse-drawn cart. 'They were using ladders as stretchers. The bodies were piled up in the cart – head to tail – until they were two layers high. The driver, a young man whom I did not recognise, jumped onto the front seat ready to drive off with his gruesome load.' He remembered the dark humour of the time as the driver looked at the bodies left behind as there was no room in the cart and said, 'Don't run away now.'

What they had seen shocked them to the core, and they returned to their temporary home, though none of them could sleep afterwards. It was not until the beginning of May when they could finally return to the school and their home next to it, and begin the process of cleaning it up:

> The dirty straw was removed from the school's two small classrooms and disposed of. The clean, unused straw was stored in the garage because it was too good to throw away. The garage stood far back in the garden and faced away from the house towards a side road. It had been hit by a shell that had caused the walls to collapse. The roof rested on the garage doors and the rear window frame, like a slightly raised chicken

coop. The only entry was through the rear window opening and there was limited space left inside which we filled with the unused straw. This tiny space would later save a human life. We also put on display all the household items which the Germans had dragged into the house and invited the neighbours to come and reclaim their belongings. We, the children, had to wash up an enormous pile of dirty plates and cutlery, something our uninvited guests had overlooked to do when they left.

On 7 May, which was Verhoeven's thirteenth birthday, he received the best of all possible presents. News arrived that the war would end officially on the following day. He walked with his cousin that day across the island toward Oosterend, but found the journey eerie as they expected to find still more unburied bodies.

Leaflets were dropped from aircraft to inform the German garrison and the Dutch population that the war was finished. The Dutch put ribbons with the country's royal colours on their clothing.

But for the Georgians on Texel the war was not yet over.

The only areas on the island which the Georgians now controlled were near De Koog on the island's west coast and De Slufter in the north. The rebels had re-sited the minefields, creating a barrier between them and the Germans. They holed up in well-camouflaged hiding places which local civilians had helped them with. The Germans dared not cross the minefields, and were in any event convinced that very few Georgians could have survived their relentless march across the island as well as the shelling.

In one incident remembered by resistance leader Keijzer, 'The Germans based at the airport captured a young Georgian. They wanted to take him away and hang him as a deserter.' This was *after* the German surrender in the Netherlands. The young Georgian

> ...was made to stand with his hands behind the back of his head but he produced a revolver and shot one of the Germans. As the Georgian fled, another German shot him through the lung. Nevertheless, he was able to make it back to his comrades and... survived thanks to Dr Veening.

Following this incident the Georgians understandably wanted to take revenge. One hundred of them – nearly half of the survivors still on Texel – 'prepared to march on the airport to confront the 200 Germans there'. Keijzer remembered that he 'was ordered to keep the two sides apart' which he managed to do 'in the nick of time'. He got the two sides to agree that the Germans could go outside only during the day and the Georgians could go out at night.[16]

The Last Victim

In the days and weeks following the German surrender on the mainland, Dutch civilians on Texel played a key role in keeping alive the Georgians who had survived the month-long battle. One of those who helped was a baker, Theo Smit.

His help to the Georgian rebels began even before the battle had started. On the afternoon of 5 April, some Georgians – then still apparently loyal soldiers of the Wehrmacht – brought him forty kilograms of flour and asked him to make bread for them. They came back to collect the bread at 9 p.m., just four hours before the beginning of 'Operation Day of Birth'.

Smit's support for the Georgians continued throughout the long weeks of the uprising, and a considerable amount of the bread he baked during that period was for Georgians who were hiding out in various parts of the island. Smit's contact with the Georgians was through one of their soldiers, Varlam Lomidze. Lomidze had been a history teacher in Tbilisi, and was captured by the Germans during the fighting in Crimea.

Smit's wife said of Lomidze:

> He was a very modest, civil boy. Actually, I can say that about all the boys who came to the shop. Never impolite or rude, and never answering me back. Varlam was hiding on a farm with four comrades, and on May 17 he and the farmer came to thank us for everything that we had done. Of course he knew our family, and wanted to know how everyone was doing. We were sitting around the kitchen table and there were even cigarettes.

The war on Texel was very nearly over and for the first time the Georgians could relax with the local Dutch population without fear. But as Mrs Smit told it, things then went terribly wrong:

> Someone said to Varlam that he did not need his revolver any more. Varlam disagreed, saying he had captured the weapon and would need it if he came across any Germans.

Even at this point, twelve days after the German surrender in the Netherlands and nine days after VE-Day, Lomidze was still concerned that if he came across any Germans, he might need to defend himself. The incident at the airport had confirmed that the situation was still dangerous. It would take several more days until the Allies finally arrived and disarmed the Germans, making it completely safe for the Georgians.

Mrs Smit continued with her story: 'My husband had always disliked weapons and asked Varlam to put the gun away, saying he was scared to death of the things. Varlam agreed and said he would unload the gun. To show that there were no bullets left in it, he pulled the trigger and shot my husband.' The panic that followed, she said, was 'indescribable'. They called Dr Veening, 'but the injury was too serious. My husband died the next morning at 2:30 a.m. But even on his death bed, he reminded me that I should continue giving food to the Georgians.'

As Mrs Smit remembered years later:

> I was grief stricken. My husband – like so many more on the island – had done a lot for the Georgians. I also felt sorry for the Georgian boy who had to live with such a guilty feeling. He wandered around the house in a daze for days after the shooting. Years afterwards, I couldn't stop thinking about this boy, who had to carry such a burden with him for the rest of his life. I wrote to him that I had forgiven him. He answered that he was indescribably grateful and that the entire Soviet population would forever be grateful to us for what we had done.[17]

Theo Smit, the baker of Texel, who died on 18 May 1945, was probably the last victim in the final battle of the Second World War in Europe.

Chapter 12

Where Were the Allies?

The Allies learned about the Georgian uprising on Texel very quickly due to the efforts of the legendary code-breakers at Bletchley Park who could read many top secret German reports without the Germans suspecting. In a signal intercepted on 6 April – as the rebellion was beginning – they decoded this message:

> The Georgian Inf. Bn. 822 on the island of Texel has mutinied. German cadre personnel appear to have been overcome. Further details not to hand. Otherwise no special incidents.[1]

It is not clear how quickly the contents of this message reached Field Marshal Montgomery and the other commanders of the British and Canadian forces in the Netherlands.

The Georgian rebels themselves planned to contact the Allies by radio, but on the day of the uprising they discovered that the broadcasting station they had hoped to use was destroyed, thereby dashing their chances of quickly receiving Allied support. Nevertheless, thanks to Ultra, the Allies were getting fairly regular updates on the rebellion – though the Georgians could not have known this.

On 11 April, the report produced by the interrogators at Kempton Park who had been questioning the Georgians on the *Joan Hodshon* from Texel confirmed the news of the uprising. 'The Germans ... were soon disposed of,' they had been told, and the Georgians were proceeding 'with mopping up operations in which they were greatly assisted by the local Dutch population'.[2]

It was an optimistic report, as the German counter-attack had not yet started in full force at the time the men on the lifeboat left Texel. The

Georgian commanders on Texel knew full well that without Allied help, they ran the risk of defeat. They had been very specific about what the men on the lifeboat were to seek from the British: 'They were instructed to ask primarily for RAF action against the German artillery.'

Nearly a week had passed during which the Georgians and their Dutch allies fought alone on Texel against massively superior German forces. Thanks both to decrypted messages coming from Bletchley Park and the interrogation of the Georgians at Kempton Park, the Allied commanders now knew what was taking place on the island. But there is no evidence that the RAF went into action against the German artillery, though there are reports of a single reconnaissance mission. No Allied forces were diverted towards Texel to help relieve the pressure on the embattled Georgians.

On 17 April, more than ten days after the outbreak of the rebellion, the code-breakers at Bletchley Park intercepted and decrypted another message about Texel which was sent to the German high command by local officers:

> Extremely fierce fighting against the enemy who is putting up a tenacious defence from strongpoint to strongpoint. Success only possible if all available artillery and other heavy weapons are employed. There are at the moment still three strongpoints in the centre, and two in the northern part of the island in the hands of the mutineers.[3]

Despite the Germans' acknowledgement that the Georgians were fighting tenaciously and that they still held some key strongpoints – including the lighthouse – the tide had already turned. With just eighteen days left of the war in the Netherlands, the Germans were winning one of their last victories of the Second World War, crushing the Georgian insurgents on Texel.

As Grisha Baindurashvili later recalled,

> The German army was reinforced. There were 800 of us and then the Germans added another 10,000 soldiers. They all came from the western front. From places where the Americans and

British could have invaded. And they attacked us. We couldn't stop them, because it was 50 against 1.

One can sense the bitterness in his words, spoken decades after the end of the war, as he blamed the Americans and British for allowing the Germans to launch their counter-attack on Texel.

Thanks to the decrypted German radio messages, it was now becoming clearer to the Allies that the fighting on Texel was coming to an end, and that the Germans were regaining control of the island. On 24 April, this appeared in secret Allied papers: 'The last strongpoint of the mutineers on Texel was reported taken on 21st April.'[4]

On 27 April, with the Georgian uprising crushed and the Germans reclaiming the island and mopping up any lingering resistance, Montgomery finally acted. He ordered II Canadian Corps, then commanded by Lt.-Gen. Guy Simonds, to capture the Wadden Islands. Texel is the largest and southern-most of these. But the request from the Canadians for commando brigades to assist in this assault was refused. According to Canadian military historian Terry Copp, 'The low priority attached to Canadian operations was evident to all.'[5]

In the end, no Allied forces landed on Texel until nearly two weeks after the German surrender.

Eventually, Soviet propagandists would make much of this, claiming that the failure of the British and Canadians to intervene was deliberate. But it seems that the western part of the Netherlands in general, and Texel in particular, were not priorities for Allied forces who had another job to do. Their route towards northern Germany took them through the eastern part of the Netherlands, and in their haste to bring a swift end to the war, they left German forces in control of large parts of Europe including the Dutch Wadden Islands. In most cases, that meant simply a continuation of a relatively peaceful status quo, as the German occupiers and the Dutch civilians impatiently waited for the war to end.

But on Texel, the fighting continued.

Chapter 13

Liberation

German claims of victory notwithstanding, the Georgian soldiers remained a thorn in their side and continued their fight long after Germany had surrendered to the Allies. It is worth recalling that, back in May 1940, the Dutch Army had fought for just five days against the invaders. In 1943, the Jewish resistance in the Warsaw Ghetto, vastly outnumbered by the Germans, battled for nearly a full month – more than most European countries did in 1940 – until they were crushed. The Georgians on Texel – with support from the local population – stood up against overwhelming German forces for more than six weeks, and never surrendered.

As he awaited the arrival of the victorious Allies, Artemidze used the opportunity to try to create a branch of the Communist Party on the island. It is unlikely that he had much success.[1] But his other project proved far more successful: starting the process of rehabilitating the Georgian soldiers of the 822nd Battalion. He collected statements from the Dutch resistance and the Communist Party confirming that the Georgians were brave fighters. 'As [an] experienced politician, he knew how important such information would be on arrival back in the Soviet Union.'[2]

'A Musical Comedy Situation'

The first Allied soldier to set foot on Texel appears to have been Siem de Waal, from the Princess Irene Brigade (a Free Dutch unit serving with the main Allied armies). According to locals, de Waal who was from Texel, had come to visit relatives on the island. Texel was still in German hands when he visited. De Waal had apparently gone off to Africa long before the war, returning in uniform. As one civilian recalled, 'He visited his relatives in his uniform ... We never saw any liberators. We heard that a few had appeared.'³

But the Canadians were on their way. One of them, Alex Rezanowich, was serving with the 1st Survey Regiment of the Royal Canadian Artillery (RCA). Rezanowich recorded his account of the Texel uprising for the Memory Project, an initiative of Historica Canada. For Rezanowich, as for millions of others, the war had ended on 8 May, celebrated as VE-Day. For his regiment, the war was supposed to be over. An official regimental history ended with these words: 'On the 8th of May we did our famous Victory March. Never was there a more feted convoy, as the Regiment moved up through Amsterdam to Beverwijk to take part in the disarming of the German Twenty-Fifth Army that had been captured in West Holland.'⁴

But, as he recalled many years after the war, a couple of weeks after the fighting in the Netherlands had ended:

> We learned that the survey regiment had another job to do before the war was over. This was on the island of Texel, where there were still armed Germans fighting a group of Russians, or Georgians, who had rebelled. This was May 20th, something like two weeks after [the] armistice.⁵

The war diary of Alex's unit, a copy of which is held by the Royal Canadian Artillery Museum in Shilo, Manitoba, has the following extraordinary entry for 17 May, nine days after VE-Day.

'C.O. Lt-Col W. D. Kirk with Capt D. R. Fletcher on recce of Texel Island,' it began. William Douglas Kirk, who commanded the first Allied forces to land on Texel, was a distinguished Canadian officer. A university-educated engineer, Kirk was forty-two years old when he first set foot on the island. By that time, he had spent nearly six years in Europe. Kirk was noted for his 'keenness, initiative and leadership,' and was awarded an OBE for his work.

According to his report on 17 May 1945,

> There are on the island about 900 Germans, mostly marines, and about 250 Russians who have mutinied and deserted from the German Army. They are still fighting together spasmodically.

> Our job would seem to be: (1) Give Russians protection from Germans while they recover wounded personnel from a mine field. (2) Give Germans protection from Russians while they are evacuated. (3) Try to get Russians evacuated. At present they an [sic] underground and are not willing to go without arms.

Clearly astonished at what he found on Texel, he added: 'It would seem to be a musical comedy situation.'

His report concluded by saying that 'Major C. R. Crocker is going over with 100 men tomorrow to do what he can.' The following day, the regiment's war diary records that 'Q' Battery had landed on the island and begun the evacuation of the Germans. On the 19th, three boatloads of Germans were taken off Texel.[6]

Alex Rezanowich who served under Lt.-Col. Kirk remembered those days well:

> Now these Georgians were prisoners, captured on the Eastern Front. They were so badly treated, beaten, starved and so on, that some of them volunteered to join the army as non-combatants.
>
> Sometime in early April, the Germans broke their promise and wanted to send the Georgian battalion which was on Texel at this time to fight the advancing Canadians. This caused a rebellion and they killed a large number of Germans in a surprise night raid. The Germans brought in reinforcements from the mainland and defeated the rebels. And the rest of the Georgians who were still alive then took to the countryside and carried on a vicious guerrilla war, where neither side took any prisoners.
>
> So when we came on the scene around May the 20th, there were still bullets flying between the Germans and the Georgians. And the Georgians were helped by the Dutch resistance and the Dutch civilians on the island.[7]

A day later, the Canadians' mission on Texel was nearly over, with the war diary stating 'Evacuation of Germans from Texel complete and will start on Russians tomorrow.'

And not a moment too soon, either, as the Germans had lost none of their swagger. One local civilian recalled the meeting between the Dutch resistance and Lt.-Col. Kirk:

> Jaap Keijzer was a commander in the resistance. He received the Canadian lieutenant-colonel. A whole platoon of Germans, all neat and tidy, arrived. They wanted to leave, of course, so they figured they'd start a provocation. Rifles under their arms. They marched past singing and all. That lieutenant-colonel nearly choked on his moustache from anger. The next day the Germans had gone. We were happy.[8]

Before they left, the Germans had a few more things to do on Texel. As Major Breitner recalled,

> My battalion was considered non-existent and the last few of our comrades were gathered together. We had already destroyed files, maps and regulations in accordance with standing orders. Finally, we burned the battalion flag 'Queen Tamara' to express our contempt for the Georgians.[9]

That flag had been presented to the Georgian soldiers serving in the 822nd Battalion two years earlier. It was a final insult.

In addition Breitner claimed, 'We also learned that some Georgians had come out of hiding from behind the minefields. The Canadians treated them with contempt.' But that may not be an entirely accurate account.

Decades later, Alex Rezanowich remembered those days on Texel rather differently:

> Our job was to restore peace and get the German army out of Texel, without any delay. When we arrived there, there were no incidents at all. Everyone was very glad to see us. Especially the Germans. The next day, the German forces were rounded up and promptly escorted to the ferry and then to the mainland where another group of our people shunted them off on their way to Germany.

The Georgians then came out of hiding and were very glad to see us. They were a friendly bunch and we had no troubles with them. I tried to speak to some of them by sign language and so on, but ... and I got the impression that they didn't want to go back to Russia. There were only something like just over two hundred survivors left after the battle.

The next day was the 22nd. Some Dutch officials came over from the mainland and they were looking for mass graves of Dutch civilians who had been killed by the Germans. They dug up two mass graves in our area, which I witnessed, but none of these were Dutch. They were all Georgian soldiers.

We left Texel a few days later, and that was that.

It's still a mystery to me why the Canadian military waited until May – until late May – to send the Survey Regiment to Texel. Because we were free after VE-Day, and all we were doing was sending Germans on their way to Germany. As a footnote to all this, we understood that the Russians didn't take kindly to prisoners of war that were being returned, and many of them were killed or jailed, sent to Siberia and so on. So the Georgians weren't too happy about returning, I suppose.

Sixty years after the war, journalist Murray Campbell interviewed Joe Bernier, another Canadian soldier, for the *Globe and Mail* newspaper. Bernier was a soldier in the 1st Survey Regiment and, according to this account, 'He played a central role in defusing a bloody battle between German soldiers and rebellious German conscripts, nearly two weeks after VE-Day.' Bernier told the interviewer: 'They said there were some Germans with a problem, that's all we knew.' The regiment's main job was to get the Germans off the island as quickly as possible. 'They went pretty nicely, considering what they'd been through and what we'd been through.'[10]

The regiment's war diary for those days ended with a different type of entry, reflecting the fact that the war had been over everywhere else for nearly a fortnight: 'Trouble in scraping up a sports team to compete in RCA meet tomorrow.'

Repatriation

Now with the Germans finally gone, it was time for the Georgians to leave Texel.

The Allies sent John Norman Stuart Buchan, 2nd Baron Tweedsmuir, to supervise the removal of the men from the island. Buchan was the son of the famous novelist John Buchan, author of *The Thirty-Nine Steps* and other popular works of fiction. John Buchan had been the Governor-General of Canada in 1935–40; his son was serving in the Canadian Army when he was given the task of dealing with the Georgians on Texel.

It's not entirely clear, however, that he was fully in command of the facts of the situation in which he found himself. In an article which he wrote for *Country Life* magazine and which appeared on 31 August 1945, he summarised the events which brought him to Texel:

> The Germans considered Texel a strategic point and built a strong coast-defence battery at either end of the island. In the flat ground in the centre they built a fighter airfield. The infantry garrison was a large one and included some 750 Russians [*sic*] who had been taken prisoner and pressed into the German Army.

Throughout the article, Tweedsmuir continued to refer to the 'Russians' on Texel. Presumably, he understood the terms 'Russian' and 'Soviet' to be interchangeable, though it's odd that he never questioned the fact that the men he found on the island wore patches on their uniforms with the word – in Latin letters – '*Georgien*'.

> About a month before VE-Day the Russians rose against the Germans and in a single night slew the entire German garrison except the gunners in the shore batteries who were inaccessible behind mines and barbed wire. One German officer escaped that night and reached the mainland.

That officer, of course, was the battalion commander, Major Breitner.

> He returned next day with more than a thousand reinforcements and some tanks. For a month an epic battle raged, in

The Vlasov Revolt

On 5 May, the same day that German forces put down their weapons nearly everywhere in the Netherlands, over 700 kilometres away events were unfolding that revealed one possible future for the surviving Georgian soldiers on Texel.

The 1st Division of the Russian Liberation Army (known by its Russian initials as ROA), was marching south through Germany. The ROA was part of something called the 'Russian Liberation Movement' whose founder was former Red Army Lieutenant-General Andrey Andreyevich Vlasov. Years earlier, Vlasov had risen steadily in the ranks of the Red Army until he was finally put in charge of one of Stalin's 'shock armies' and entrusted with the defence of Kiev during the German invasion.*

When his army was encircled and destroyed, Vlasov was captured by the Germans. While a prisoner of war he switched sides and agreed to support the German war effort. He founded and led the Russian Liberation Movement which aimed to free Russia from Stalinist rule and negotiate 'peace with honour' with the Third Reich. The Germans didn't entirely trust Vlasov, and the top Nazi leadership, in particular Hitler, did not approve of working with 'racially inferior' Slavs. So it wasn't until November 1944, with the Third Reich's defeat now certain, that Vlasov's 'Russian Liberation Army', armed and equipped by the Germans, was finally allowed to take to the field.

The other Soviet nationalities that found themselves on the German side during the war were suspicious of Vlasov and his army, though for different reasons. The Georgians who were fighting for the Germans showed little interest in working with him. But General

---

* A good source of information about Vlasov's army is Catherine Andreyev, *Vlasov and the Russian Liberation Movement: Soviet Reality and Emigré Theories*. Other good sources are Alexander Dallin, *German Rule in Russia* and George Fischer, *Soviet Opposition to Stalin*.

Shalva Maglakelidze, who had commanded the Georgian Legion for a time, was personally sympathetic to the Vlasovites.

In the few months remaining in the war, Vlasov's Russians were increasingly at odds with their German allies, and were keen to get as close as possible to Western Allied lines, hoping that they could surrender to the Americans rather than the Soviets. They had no expectation of mercy from the Soviets. Some hoped that with the end of the war with Nazi Germany, the Western Allies would continue the fight against Soviet Russia – a belief shared by German propaganda minister Goebbels. If a Third World War were to break out, Vlasov's men expected that they would be welcomed as allies by the Americans in their fight against the Soviet Union.

In Prague, the capital of Czechoslovakia (the first country to fall victim to German aggression in 1938), the hated German occupiers were still in charge, even in early May 1945. The local population rose up in rebellion – but met fierce German resistance. The Germans sent Waffen-SS units to level the city.

The leaders of that uprising initially welcomed the arrival on the scene of Vlasov's Russians who they assumed (correctly) had disobeyed German orders. Groups of Czech partisans came to Vlasov asking for supplies, and for his agreement to cooperate in the fight against the Germans. There are reports that some of these partisans even offered Vlasov the leadership of their rebellion. But this goodwill soon slipped away as it became clearer to the Czechs that with the approach of the Soviet forces, Vlasov and his army had become toxic.

There were some initial clashes between the ROA and German forces before the real battle began. This occurred in part due to pressure from the rank and file, who had been growing increasingly hostile to the Germans and sympathetic to the welcoming Czechs.

Some Vlasovites were definitely thinking along the same lines as the Georgians on Texel. They were keen to prove to the Allies that they were not on the side of the Germans, and that instead they were victims. And maybe some of them felt that turning their arms against the Germans, even at this late stage in the war, might help persuade the Soviets to treat them with some leniency. On 5 May Vlasov's army reached the outskirts of Prague and the battle against the Germans began in earnest the following day.

Later, when some of Vlasov's men met representatives of the newly formed Soviet-backed Czech government, two-thirds of whose members were Communists, the Czechs announced that they had not asked Vlasov for help and did not sympathise with his cause. No doubt the rapid advance of the Soviet forces towards Prague helped influence their change of heart. They also distanced themselves from the organisers of the uprising in the city. They encouraged the ROA to surrender to the Red Army when it reached Prague.

About half of Vlasov's division, 10,000 men, were captured by the Red Army, some directly, and some by Czech partisans who turned them over. The other half reached the American lines, though many of these were later forcibly repatriated to the Soviet Union. Eventually Vlasov himself, who had refused the offer of a flight to safety in Spain, was captured as well.

Nothing was heard of him for over a year, until 2 August 1946 when it was announced in *Izvestia*, the Soviet government's daily newspaper, that he and eleven of his comrades had been tried on charges of treason by the Military Tribunal of the USSR's Supreme Court. They were found guilty and were all hanged.

By early May 1945, the Georgians on Texel had been reduced to hiding in ditches and farmyards, as the Germans hunted them down, and were unlikely to have been aware of the events unfolding in Prague. Had they known, it might have undermined their belief that by taking on the Germans they were somehow redeeming themselves in the eyes of the Soviets.

Taking up arms against the Germans in the last days of the war didn't save the lives of Vlasov and his closest associates. Would the surviving Georgians on Texel be treated any differently?

which the Russians, heavily outnumbered and shelled not only from the Texel batteries but from the mainland as well resisted stubbornly. VE-Day came just in time to save them.

Actually, as we now know, VE-Day did not come in time to save them, and the Germans continued hunting down the Georgians for another twelve days past VE-Day. It is this fact that makes the battle on Texel the last battle of the Second World War in Europe.

Most of Tweedsmuir's 1945 article is actually about the birds he spotted on Texel, and is accompanied by photographs of some of these. As he explained in a book written eight years later, 'An abiding interest in birds had always given me a special wish to visit two places in Europe,' and one of these was Texel – which was 'referred to so frequently in all my bird books . . . the tide of war bore me to Texel in the course of duty'.[11]

In that account of his visit, he provided more detail about his dealings with the Georgian survivors on Texel:

> Somebody had to parley with them, and the job fell to me. It was not a very easy parley, for many of them, to show their independence, would fire their rifles up in the air and not always upwards. But in the end an agreement was worked out by which, if they laid down their arms, they would be conveyed to the nearest Russian authority, who was a Russian liaison officer in Wilhelmshaven in Germany. I was to go with them, to explain to the Russian authorities that they had been forced into the German Army against their will, but had since struck a valiant blow against their country's enemy. In short, I was to testify that the colour of their uniforms was not their fault, and that they deserved well of their own people.[12]

The Georgians meanwhile were preparing to depart Texel. They held their final parade on the island in front of the offices of the ferry company. As the Georgians waited in Oudeschild harbour, many Texelians came by to say their goodbyes. Gongladze and Artemidze made speeches – which were presumably translated into Dutch – thanking the local people and apologising for all the suffering their rebellion had caused. They were applauded.

Tweedsmuir remembered going with 'three other Canadian officers in a motor-boat from Den Helder to Texel. It was going to be a hot day and the morning sun was shining and sparkling on the waves. A good-sized vessel, the Texel ferry-boat, was lying in the little harbour.' The ferry was the *Dokter Wagemaker*.

> The Russians were lined up on the quay with their weapons. After a great deal of delay, and further parley, we persuaded them to embark not many minutes before the falling tide would have stranded the ferry. They enlivened the short trip to Den Helder by throwing potato-masher grenades overboard, and occasionally firing their weapons.
>
> On the quay at Den Helder, a trim company of Princess Patricia's Canadian Light Infantry were awaiting us. After the Russians had surrendered their weapons, we conducted an intensive search and removed nine more automatic pistols concealed in various folds of their garments.
>
> The whole of that long summer's day, our convoy of trucks wound along the roads. The guards were relieved at two points, farther on, by companies of other Canadian regiments. It was nearly dark when we reached our destination, and we parleyed with a Russian colonel with one eye and, apparently, the basic minimum of human intellect. I handed over to him a document, signed by our Canadian general, attesting to the feats of arms of these men on the Allied side. The chief of Texel Russians told me that he was perfectly satisfied that everything reasonable had been done, and that his country would receive him and his comrades back to the fold. He thanked me warmly for my help, and I shook hands with his officers. I was told afterwards that these unfortunate people were butchered to a man.[13]

While the Germans leaving Texel were keen to get home to their families, the Georgians who survived what Tweedsmuir called an 'epic battle' faced their future back home with some trepidation. Would they be welcomed as heroes of the fight against fascism? Would they be punished for their treason to the Soviet Union? No one knew.

'A Brave and Dauntless Ally'

It is hard to date the beginning of the myth of the Texel uprising.

Perhaps it began on that day in April 1945, when Shalva Loladze ordered Dutch civilians to report to him, and explained to them that the rebellion on Texel was part of a much larger action across the Netherlands. It was nothing of the sort, and he knew that. The announcement to the Dutch that Texel had been liberated, that it was time for local people to take out the national flags and celebrate, was certainly part of the myth creation. These soldiers of the Georgian Legion, the 822nd Eastern Battalion, were being transformed even as the battle was raging into an integral part of the victorious Allied forces. They were playing their role in the Great Patriotic War, the Soviet name for the Second World War.

Two documents written by top Allied commanders certainly contributed to the creation of the myth of Texel. The first was a message addressed to 'to whom it may concern' by Lt.-Gen. Charles Foulkes, commander of I Canadian Corps, dated 16 June 1945 – 'in the field'. It is worth reprinting in full as it gives what the Allied command understood at that point to have happened on Texel – and the message they were conveying to the Soviet leadership. This is the message that Tweedsmuir delivered to the 'Russian colonel with one eye and, apparently, the basic minimum of human intellect':

> In connection with the movement of 226 Soviet soldiers from Texel Island to the Russian camp near Wilhelmshaven, it is desired to bring to the attention of the Soviet High Command the assistance received by Canadian tps from this group from the 6 Apr 45 to the capitulation.
>
> Prior to 6 Apr 45, this group contacted Dutch NBS [Partisans] and worked closely with them. Three times important messages were sent to British Gov and three replies received. On instructions from NBS, this group removed German mines from important coastal areas on Texel Island, arranging signs in such a way that the Germans did not know of their removal. This act was invaluable later when Canadians landed on the

Island. In addition to this, arms and information were given to the NBS.

When on 6 Apr 45, this group was ordered to fight the English, they rose up against the Germans and the 700 Georgians fought 4000 Germans for three days. During this period Dutch, Soviet and British flags were displayed throughout the Island. The Germans then bombarded the island from Den Helder with heavy weapons, resulting in much damage being done to buildings and considerable casualties to civilians. The Germans then landed tanks, mortars and heavy weapons, and the Soviet group withdrew to prepare defensive positions from which they withstood every German onslaught for over a month, when, with ammunition gone, their Commander ordered them to break out in small groups and carry on the fight as partisans. This lasted until 21 May 45, when Canadian troops landed on the Island. The Soviet tps then assisted the Canadians to round up and disarm the remaining Germans, and were permitted to retain weapons for their protection.

During the course of the above engagements, the Soviet Gp sustained casualties amounting to 470 killed, 13 seriously wounded, and 40 others wounded. The German casualties are estimated at about 2347. It is significant to note that after the enemy capitulated, the Soviet group sustained about 200 casualties when assisting to round up the enemy tps. These are included in the casualty figures given above.

It is felt that the assistance rendered to the Allied Cause generally, and the 1st Canadian Corps in particular, by this group was of inestimable value. The great courage displayed against overwhelming odds when ordered to fight against the Allies, and the determined will to resist to the last, despite their desperate position at that time is to be highly commended.

Since the cessation of hostilities this group has remained on the Island pending arrangements for their return, and displayed a spirit of discipline and behaviour which would be a credit to any corps. An excellent spirit of co-operation with Canadian

HQ has pervaded in all dealings with us and in spite of the fact that it is their misfortune to have to wear the despised uniform of the enemy, we feel that they are entitled to all the honours of a brave and dauntless Ally.[14]

A month later, echoing Foulkes's message, General Eisenhower, Supreme Commander of Allied forces in Europe, sent a secret cipher telegram to '30 Military Mission' in Moscow. It is an extraordinary document which is today buried deep in one of the folders in the National Archives in Kew, and it reads as follows:

> Have received report from Dutch concerning revolt by Georgians on Texel Island. In view substance this report which shows Georgians fought extremely hard in attempt to overcome Germans you may wish to pass following information to Russians.
>
> 1. On night 5/6 April Georgians killed all German officers on Texel. Lower ranks prevented from doing any harm.
>
> 2. 6th April Georgians occupied whole island. German attempt to land from Den Helder failed but heavy artillery from Den Helder caused Georgians' withdrawal to northern-most part of island.
>
> 3. Later 200 Germans landed Oudeschild suffering heavy losses.
>
> Artillery fire continued 7/8 April. SS troops landed 8/9. On 10th April Georgians fortified themselves behind wide minefields. Germans considered position very strong. Panzers brought in.[15]

The reference to 'report from Dutch concerning revolt' is intriguing as no such report appears in the files in the National Archives in Kew.

Several months later, a letter from Thomas Brimelow in the British Foreign Office made reference to Eisenhower's message. Brimelow was a British diplomat who was involved in the forced repatriation to the Soviets and their allies of Cossacks and others who had fought on the German side. Writing on 30 November, Brimelow noted that,

Some months ago we were asked by the Soviet Embassy here whether we could supply them with full details of the rising of Soviet prisoners of war against the Germans on the Dutch Island of Texel, which broke out on the 5th April last. All that we were able to promise, however, was a copy of a report based on the interrogation of 4 Georgians who took part in the revolt, and who were subsequently despatched to this country to appeal for help.

The report based on that interrogation has been quoted already. But in addition Brimelow said:

> SHAEF were at the time in possession of a Dutch report on the insurrection, which may well contain much more information than we were able to supply. If so, we should like to consider the desirability either of passing a copy of this report to the Soviet Embassy here – as a gesture of friendliness – or of telling them we understand that the Dutch are in possession of a fuller report on the incident.
>
> In the first place, however, we should wish to see the report in question ourselves.[16]

Chapter 14

Back in the USSR

The surviving Georgians had every reason to regard their return to the USSR with apprehension.

In telling the story of the rebellious Georgians in the French town of Hirson who had killed their German officers and joined the French resistance, Christian de Groote ended by saying, 'As for the Georgians, after being relieved of weapons, they were escorted to a Mediterranean port, Toulon or Marseilles, from when they must sail to Odessa. On disembarking in the USSR they had all been shot without trial.'[1]

It has been reported that of 8,000 Georgians who served in the German Army, about half were repatriated to the Soviet Union by the Western Allies. Donald Rayfield painted a bleak picture of their fate:

> A Georgian nurse, Tina Balanchivadze, married to a German officer, was forcibly parted from her husband and child and sent to the Gulag. Some Georgians were shot by SMERSH [the Red Army's counter-intelligence agency] on the spot, most were consigned to the Gulag; few returned to civilian life or found asylum... On 12 November 1951 Kandid Charkviani told Stalin that 5,897 Georgian POWs with family members, 190 repatriated émigrés, 433 relatives and 2,644 illegal entrants were sent to the camps.[2]

Compared to most, the Georgians who survived the uprising on Texel got lucky. It appears that on their arrival in the Soviet Union, they were not shot. Instead, most of them were given jobs as construction workers for the Red Army for the first few months. During those months, their cases were reviewed. In early 1946, they finally made it back home to Tbilisi.

According to Gongladze,

> Before returning home we served several months in the Soviet Army. We were warmly welcomed when we arrived at the border because the army newspapers all reported extensively on our rebellion. Everybody knew about us and we were idolized. The generals also really respected us.[3]

Initially, it appeared that most of the returnees were not to be punished at all. Some may have been arrested in 1948 and exiled for a time. Some researchers place the number sent off to the Gulag at around thirty, a small fraction of the more than 200 who returned alive from Texel. It has been suggested that one, maybe more, died there. There do not appear to have been wholesale executions – let alone men being shot without trial after disembarking from their boats, as some reports would have it. Tweedsmuir's comment that 'these unfortunate people were butchered to a man' was not true.

The treatment of some of the Texel veterans seems extremely lenient indeed. According to reports, a number of the returnees from Texel were punished by being exiled to Baku, the capital of neighbouring Azerbaijan. This was so close to home, to Georgia, that the families of the men could easily come and visit them. There are stories that some of the men just walked back to Georgia eventually.[4] By 1956, all the Texel veterans who had been exiled or punished in any other way were rehabilitated by the new Soviet leadership which had taken charge following Stalin's death three years earlier.

Different veterans told different stories of their treatment after their return home at the end of the war. Grisha Baindurashvili, for example, told an interviewer,

> We returned to our homeland only a year later, after spending time in one prison camp after another. Then we heard that KGB was looking for us, but they never found us among the masses of prisoners. Soon afterwards we were taken to a meeting with two Georgian colonels, Kurashvili and Khuberaishvili, who brought us our renewed ID papers.[5]

Evgeni Artemidze returned to Georgia and studied law in Tbilisi. He later managed an academic publishing house in the Georgian capital. He married in 1949 and had two daughters. Eventually he returned to Manglisi, a town not far from the village where he was born.

Probably the strangest case of all was that of General Shalva Maglakelidze, the former commander of the Georgian Legion, who did not get along very well with his German commanders and had eventually been removed from his post.

When the war ended, Maglakelidze was not repatriated to the USSR, as were most members of the Georgian Legion. He wound up in West Germany where he worked as a military advisor to Chancellor Konrad Adenauer. On 26 January 1954, he founded the 'Union of Georgian Soldiers Abroad' in Munich, and seven months later, in August of that year, he was kidnapped by KGB agents in West Germany.

In most cases, that would be the end of the story. Traitors to the Soviet motherland who were captured by the security services and returned to the USSR did not generally have happy fates. But Maglakelidze was allowed to return home to Georgia after many decades living abroad.

In the years following Stalin's death, the Soviets were keen to entice some expatriates to return, and they used the case of Maglakelidze in their propaganda to show how lenient they were to those who made their way home. They also used Maglakelidze in their ongoing efforts to discredit and divide the Georgian émigré community. The state-controlled Soviet media published a 'confession' by Maglakelidze in which he called the émigrés agents of Western intelligence services. He also at one point announced that he regretted the crimes he had committed against his motherland. Maglakelidze was permitted to live and work in Tbilisi under the watchful eyes of the Soviet secret police until his death in 1976.

Not only were the Texel veterans allowed to return to their homes and resume their lives in Georgia, but they were later given leave to host Dutch tourists who began to come to the country, and even permitted to travel to the Netherlands for the occasional reunion and ceremonial visit to Texel. At the height of the Cold War it was very unusual for ordinary Soviet citizens to be given the right to travel to the West.

The treatment of returning prisoners, and in particular those who had joined the German Army and fought in its ranks, was generally far from gentle. The trial and hanging of General Vlasov and his officers was not the exception, but the rule. The relative leniency of the treatment of the Georgians from Texel is something of a mystery.

Part of the explanation may lie in the letters sent by Generals Foulkes and Eisenhower to their Soviet counterparts, emphasising how, in their view, Loladze and his men were genuine allies of the anti-fascist cause. In the period before the Cold War, with memories of the wartime alliance still fresh, the Soviets may have wanted to avoid deliberately challenging Eisenhower and other Western military leaders.

The Texel veterans were assisted greatly in this by the leadership of the Dutch Communist Party, which was busily engaged in building up the heroic Georgian rebels on Texel and their local Communist allies. The Dutch Communists even produced blank documents, on Party letterhead, already stamped, asserting that the individuals were genuine anti-fascist fighters. For many years they built up the mythology of Georgian fighters on Texel, for their own reasons, but this may have resonated in the Soviet Union as well. And of course some of the Texel veterans themselves contributed to this story by emphasising their disloyalty to the Germans, and how they were essentially forced into the Legion. Those stories may have saved the lives of men like Baindurashvili and Artemidze.

There is some evidence that the Soviet authorities distinguished between Georgians who seemed more loyal to the Communist Party, such as Artemidze (who famously claimed that the uniform he wore was Hitler's – but his heart belonged to Stalin), and others. Factional differences that arose among the men on Texel continued to play a role years after the war had ended.

Some of the answers to questions about the treatment of the returning Georgian Legion veterans may be found in the archives of the Georgian KGB, which were opened to the public after the collapse of the Soviet Union and Georgia's independence. But scholars in Georgia say that a lot of material is missing or inaccessible, supposedly to protect the privacy of individuals, but possibly also to hide certain facts.

We may never know why the Georgians on Texel didn't suffer the same fate as, for example, Vlasov. What we do know is that even before they left the island, the myth-making had already begun.

Chapter 15

The Making of a Myth

The story of the creation of the myth of the Texel uprising cannot be separated from the Cold War, which broke out not long after the Second World War had ended. The Soviet Union was no longer an ally, and the Iron Curtain which came down across Europe meant that little was known in the West about the fate of the Texel Georgians. People in the Netherlands wanted to know what had become of them.

Not long after the Georgians boarded the boats in Oudeschild on their way back home, non-Communist journalists began asking about their fate. It was known that many Soviet citizens, including POWs, suffered terribly upon their return to the USSR. A year after the war ended, the fate of General Vlasov became well known when the Soviets publicised the story of his trial and execution in *Izvestia*. Due to the Yalta agreement it was understood that Stalin had demanded and received the right to do as we wished with people he and his regime had already labelled as traitors. People on Texel suspected that the Georgians faced detention or death on their return. But their fate turned out to be rather more complicated than that, as we have seen.

Meanwhile, in the Netherlands an early step in the creation of the myth was the decision to make a cemetery for the Georgians who died during their rebellion. This was done very quickly, while the Georgians were still on the island. The Georgian soldiers located mass graves across the island and got the help of local people to identify the victims and to bring them for reburial. The spot chosen for the cemetery was a beautiful meadow just south of Den Burg. As I learned on Texel, the land had been confiscated from a Dutch Nazi.[1]

The burial ceremony took place quite quickly, less than a week after the Canadians had landed, on 26 May. At that time, 187 bodies, all of them Georgians, were buried in nine rows. Once those bodies were in the ground, a ceremony took place in which the Georgians who had not yet been evacuated from the island honoured the memory of Loladze and the other men with speeches and salutes. Loladze's body was the last to be buried, at the highest point on the gentle slope.[2]

The number of those initially buried in the cemetery was only a fraction of those killed in the fighting. This was the case because at first the Georgians insisted that only those who fought to the death against the Nazis deserved the honour of a military burial. Those who chose to surrender to the Germans – and who were killed by them, often with their uniforms stripped off – were left out. The Germans had considered them traitors and the Georgians thought them cowards. Their bodies remained in anonymous mass graves. But two years later, with the support of the Soviet embassy in the Netherlands, *all* the Georgians buried on the island, no matter how they died, were given the honour of burial in the new cemetery. In the end, there were 485 graves.

Before leaving Texel, having created the cemetery that would be a memorial to their fight, the Georgians had one more job to do. On 15 June 1945, the day before they left Texel, the Georgian survivors put up a memorial at the cemetery consisting of a hammer and sickle and red star, thus demonstrating their loyalty to the Soviet regime.

There was also a photograph of their dead leader, Loladze, with this text: 'Here rests the brave Soviet captain Loladze Shalva and his brothers-in-arms who fought for their freedom against German terror on the island of Texel. We are and will remain Georgians and we will never forget our brave fallen comrades.'

Having buried their comrades and erected a monument to their memory, the Georgians could now leave the island and head home to an uncertain fate.

The memorial they left behind was initially not treated with respect by some of the locals on Texel. On several occasions, the glass was shattered by unknown vandals. Local media condemned the vandalism, declaring that whoever did it had a 'twisted soul'. Fearing further attacks on the property, the local government surrounded the cemetery with barbed wire. This caused outrage, with the local newspaper comparing the appearance of the cemetery to that of a concentration camp. The outrage spread, and even national newspapers in the Netherlands picked up on it.

The Communist Party's daily newspaper, *De Waarheid*, which was at the time the largest newspaper in the Netherlands, wrote:

> It is one of the most disgraceful expressions of neglect and ingratitude vis-à-vis fallen combatants for Dutch liberty that we have experienced so far. What will the Russians think of our civilisation, that we like to boast about so much?[3]

The reference to the Georgians on Texel as 'combatants for Dutch liberty' was an early indication of the tone that the local Communists were going to take about the rebellion. The Georgians on Texel, they would argue, had fought to free the island from the German occupiers, and were therefore heroes.

Behind the outrage regarding the barbed wire, Dutch people had mixed emotions about the Georgians buried in the cemetery. Even then, with the memory still fresh, many on Texel considered the Georgian rebellion to have been selfishly motivated and a disaster for the island and its civilian population. A local clergyman said:

> Texel civilians have been involved in the uprising partly of their own free will and partly through coercion. Since the Russians' rebellion aimed at their self-preservation, their battle was not our battle . . . It is simply foolish to think that the mutineers became 'allied fighters' because they rose up.[4]

The Dutch Communists

While many local people remained unconvinced about the heroism of the Georgian 'allies', the Dutch Communist Party, for its own reasons, demanded that the rebels be recognised as genuine heroes. The Communist Party, which had been very weak before the war, had grown enormously following the Allied victory. The Party had played a major role in the resistance, and had won the respect of many.

But the Dutch Communists also had their own skeleton in the closet: their neutrality (at best) during the first year of the German occupation, when Germany and the Soviet Union were allies. Just as the Georgians on Texel had tried to compensate for their own decision first to surrender to the Germans and then to join the German Army, both of which would have been considered treason by the Soviet state, the Dutch Communists were also making amends for their own 'lapse' in 1940–1. Their efforts to rewrite the story of the Texel rebellion were closely linked to the rewriting of their own history to cover up their own failures. The myth-building around Texel served both the Georgians now being repatriated to the Soviet Union and the Dutch Communists, who had political ambitions in the post-war Netherlands.

The Dutch Communists were not unique in this sense. Communist parties across Europe had grown enormously in numbers and prestige following the war. The Italian and French parties became serious contenders for power – and remained very strong forces for decades after the war. All the European Communist parties struggled with their legacy of collaboration with the Germans during the period of the Hitler–Stalin Pact.

The Norwegian Communists, for example, attempted to destroy all copies of their party newspaper (*Arbeideren*) from the period 1940–1. They managed to do this with a certain degree of success, removing copies from libraries across the country, but one full set of the newspapers had been taken out of Norway, and deposited in the library of Cornell University in upstate New York. Decades later, these became an invaluable resource for a Norwegian Labour Party leader – and militant anti-Stalinist – Haakon Lie. Lie was given support in this matter by his close friend, Cornell Professor Walter Galenson.[5]

In 1974, following attacks on the Norwegian Labour Party by members of the country's small Communist Party (NKP) in which the Labour Party leaders were accused of being 'untrustworthy', Lie published a small book entitled *Who Can We Trust?* It told the story of the Norwegian Communist Party's role during the Hitler–Stalin Pact years. In the book, Lie reproduced front pages and articles from *Arbeideren* during the dark days of NKP–Nazi collaboration. He summarised the role of the NKP during the war by repeating what had been said of the Finnish Communists during the Winter War with the Soviet Union in 1939–40; they were called 'Russians who spoke Finnish'. Lie said the NKP were 'Russians who spoke Norwegian'.

The Dutch Communists could equally have been called 'Russians who spoke Dutch'. They certainly had acted during the years of the Hitler–Stalin Pact less as representatives of the Dutch working class than as agents of Soviet foreign policy.

And even after the Dutch Communists were allowed to join in the fight against the Germans following the invasion of the Soviet Union, there may have also have been some concern that the Communists were not as proactive as they would have liked to have been in the underground. For a number of reasons, the Dutch resistance did not focus on armed struggle against the German occupation, unlike the partisans in Poland, or in the occupied parts of the Soviet Union or even the *maquis* in France.

It seems that the Georgians on Texel on the first night of their rebellion killed more Germans than the Dutch resistance had killed in the course of the entire war. The bloody Georgian uprising would be used by the Dutch Communists afterwards to build up their reputation as part of a more militant fight against the Germans.

The Beginning of Memorialisation

Following the fiasco of the barbed wire fence around the Georgian cemetery on Texel, and the pressure from the Dutch Communists to take the matter more seriously, the local government in Texel commissioned a proper monument to the fallen, to be designed by a known sculptor. While this process dragged on, it was decided to tidy up the cemetery and make it more beautiful. This included the planting of bushes and trees, the laying of paths, and the provision of rows of red roses instead of gravestones. A brick wall around the cemetery replaced the barbed wire. Over time the cemetery evolved from an improvised memorial site thrown up quickly in the days between the end of the fighting and the repatriation of the Georgians into a proper, tidy and orderly cemetery, like most others in Europe.

By 1946, a committee had been formed to organise an annual ceremony at the cemetery. The committee initially included a representative of the Dutch Communists, Cornelia Boon-Verberg, much loved by the veterans who called her the 'mother of the Georgians', and who would later on be honoured by them in a corner of the cemetery. Others included Wim Kelder, who had been leader of the local resistance and who was brought to Loladze on the morning the uprising began. The commander of the small Dutch post-war naval base on the island was also part of the first group to organise a memorial event.

At the event itself, held to mark the first anniversary of the uprising, a large group of some 400 people participated. Among them were representatives of the Dutch Communist Party and the newspaper *De Waarheid*. Annie van Ommeren-Averink, who had been known to the resistance as 'Annie Klein', was in attendance. She had known the Georgians when they were stationed in Zandvoort, and was their link to the local resistance. In later years, she would be blamed by some for inciting the Georgians to rebel, regardless of the consequences.

Though many representatives of civil society and even the military were in attendance, the Dutch government decided not to participate in the event. The ambassador of the Soviet Union came, with embassy staff and accompanied by the commander of the Dutch Navy. The ambassador publicly donated a cheque for 3,000 guilders to help build a permanent monument. He also laid a wreath. He spoke briefly – in Russian – and praised the rebels and the people of Texel who had died fighting 'in a battle against an enemy that tried to conquer the world with the fascist terror system'.

It is important to note the timing of this event. It was May 1946, and many of the Soviet soldiers and civilians who had been repatriated to the USSR following the end of the war, had already been sent into the Gulag, or put to death. Just a few weeks after the Texel ceremony, General Vlasov and his officers from the 'Russian Liberation Army' were condemned to death by a Soviet military court and hanged. But already now, barely a year after the war was over, the official Soviet position seemed to be that the Georgian rebels on Texel, despite their initial surrender to the Germans, and their later decision to wear the uniforms of the enemy, were actually heroic anti-fascist fighters. There was no equivocation here at all.

The Soviet leadership, together with the Dutch Communist Party, had decided that Loladze and his men had liberated Texel, and had fallen in an epic battle against the German fascists. Though the veterans of the Texel uprising, now back in the USSR, were not yet fully rehabilitated, and in many cases not even yet back in Georgia, in the Netherlands the Soviet government had already rehabilitated them. They were heroes.

The Soviet participation in the 1946 ceremony on Texel was part and parcel of an effort across Europe to ensure that the Soviet contribution to winning the war against Germany was recognised. Soviet officials appeared at many ceremonies with this end in mind. On Texel, their agenda was not the same as that of the islanders, who held a separate event afterwards in Den Burg. That ceremony, which honoured not the Georgians but the civilians and other Allied soldiers who had fallen, was denounced by *De Waarheid* which insisted that it had been organised by local 'reactionaries' trying to take attention away from the Georgians.

A battle over historical memory was already taking place, though the war had been over for only a year.

By the time of the second anniversary in 1947, the Dutch government had already decided that memorial ceremonies would take place on the evening of 4 May, designated as Dutch National Remembrance Day. The following day, 5 May, marked the end of the war in the Netherlands. Of course the war on Texel lasted another two weeks after that, but it was decided to keep to the national schedule.

On Texel, it was decided to hold a brief ceremony in the cemetery on the afternoon of 4 May before the main event in the evening. Soviet diplomats came each year to these events, and gave speeches which always referred to the men buried there as prisoners of war who had taken up arms and rebelled against the Germans who were guarding them. That they could say this such a short time after the war had ended, in the presence of people who knew that this was not the case and that the Georgians were in fact soldiers in the German Army, is astonishing. But this was the official Soviet line as early as the 1940s.

Meanwhile, the cemetery still lacked a permanent memorial to replace the temporary one erected by the Georgians before their departure in June 1945. The Soviet embassy in the Netherlands agreed on a design in November 1952, and it was unveiled in May 1953 on the eighth anniversary of the uprising. The memorial was a granite wall with the coats of arms of the Soviet Union and Texel engraved on it.

Contacts Between Texel and Georgia

While Texel was holding its two ceremonies and making changes to the cemetery at which the Georgians were honoured each May, the survivors of the Texel rebellion were not all fully rehabilitated by the regime until 1956, during the Khrushchev 'thaw' following Stalin's death in 1953. On Texel, nothing was known about their fate. There had been attempts over the course of a decade to establish contact, but to avail.

At the ceremony in May 1955, a time when the rehabilitation of the rebels in the Soviet Union was not yet complete, the military attaché of the Soviet embassy in the Netherlands read out a statement supposedly written by the veterans back home in Georgia. In the statement, they expressed their thanks to the people of Texel. But there was still no direct contact between the people of Texel and the surviving Georgians who had been escorted off the island by the Canadians in June 1945.

A full eleven years after that event, Dutch newspapers reported that a Russian-language newspaper published in Georgia, *Zary Vostoka*, had referred to the Georgians as 'keen Soviet patriots'. This meant to some that they were now rehabilitated completely. *De Waarheid* published photographs of 'Little Stalin' (Evgeni Artemidze), now back in Georgia, as well as news from there. Still, many doubted the reports that the Georgians had safely made it home without reprisals.

Meanwhile on Texel, the Cold War was taking its toll on the annual ceremony to mark the Georgian uprising. The Dutch Intelligence Service suspected Texelians who attended the event of sympathy for the Communists, and photographed them. In the paranoia of the time, local people began seeing suspicious photographers arriving from the mainland and suspected the worst. As in the USA and elsewhere during the Cold War, if one was suspected of sympathy for the Soviet Union or Communism, one ran the risk of not getting civil service jobs. As a result, over time, fewer and fewer locals attended the ceremony for the Georgians – and the Communist presence at the event grew more prominent as a result.

A full fifteen years after the revolt, reliable news about the fate of the Georgian survivors now back in the USSR finally reached the West. On the anniversary of the rebellion on 7 April, *De Waarheid* ran an article by a journalist who had interviewed eleven Georgian survivors in Tbilisi. They told him that they remembered the island well, and had written to islanders despite language problems. The Communist author pointed out that the veterans were all happy, had good jobs, and had not suffered upon their return to the USSR. The article directly countered anti-Communist propaganda which claimed that all those who were repatriated to the Soviet Union at the end of the war were sent to the camps or shot.

Shortly after the article appeared, closer relations developed between the surviving Georgians and the Texelians. Cornelia Boon-Verberg, who had done so much to help the Georgians during the uprising, finally began receiving letters from some of them, who were now back home in Georgia. In 1963, three Texelians were given recognition by the Soviets for the role they had played in 1945 – making them honorary members of the Association of Soviet War Veterans. A year later, one of the Georgian veterans came to Texel with the Soviet delegation to the May commemoration. And some of the better-known Georgian veterans, among them Artemidze and Gongladze, wrote a letter to Texel's mayor expressing their thanks.

The early 1960s was a period of relative liberalisation in the USSR, a time when Alexander Solzhenitsyn could legally publish his novella about the labour camps, *One Day in the Life of Ivan Denisovich*, while others could begin to discuss Stalin's crimes. It would not last. But while it was happening, Georgians began to be allowed to leave the country and visit Texel. Some veterans of the uprising were finally able to do this.

They would come to the cemetery on 4 May, bringing with them Georgian soil to scatter over the graves so that the men would, at least symbolically, be buried in the earth of their homeland. Despite persisting

Cold War tensions, and the difficulties of getting visas, the Georgians continued to come to visit Texel. They brought a copper plaque with an image of Loladze which would serve as a tombstone for him. Reunions between islanders and Georgian veterans were often quite emotional.

Finally, more than two decades after the uprising, Cornelia Boon-Verberg received an invitation to visit Georgia and received a warm welcome. She participated in a dinner with some 120 survivors of the uprising, talking to many of them. Tbilisi, Georgia's capital, awarded her the Freedom of the City. As she would later note, the Dutch government – unlike the Soviets – never gave any awards or recognition to her or anyone else who helped the Georgians during their rebellion.

For the Dutch, the anniversary of the Georgian uprising on Texel remained controversial for many years to come.

Chapter 16

Crucified Island

More than two decades after the uprising on Texel, the Soviet rewriting of history reached its culmination with the release of the film *Crucified Island* (*Jvartsmuli kundzuli*), in 1968. Although it was a feature film, with actors, not a documentary, Soviet audiences were meant to understand that the story it told was essentially a true one. Directed by Shota Managadze and written by Rezo Tabukashvili, it presented the rebellion as if the Georgians were prisoners of war who broke loose, somehow got their hands on weapons, and took on the Germans.

The film had its Western European premiere on Texel in April 1970. Screenwriter Rezo Tabukashvili brought a copper name board in three languages – Dutch, Georgian and Russian – to be placed in the Georgian cemetery on Texel. In translation this said, 'Communal grave of Soviet soldiers from Georgia'.

As the British Film Institute describes it, the film is 'an account of the uprising of a battalion of Georgian POWs on the Dutch island of Texel in April–May 1945. The Georgian POWs, who had been conscripted into German military service, work alongside the Dutch Resistance sabotaging German fortifications and leading an armed rebellion to take control of the island.'[1] That's a decent enough summary of the film, but those two short sentences contain several errors of fact. And these are completely in line with Soviet propaganda of the time – and continue the story initially spun as early as 1946 by the Soviet ambassador to the Netherlands at the first commemoration of the uprising on Texel.

Shot in black and white, *Crucified Island* feels to a viewer today like a film made in the 1940s, not in 1968. It has some striking cinematography, and the film-makers clearly worked hard to find somewhere, presumably in the USSR, that looked like Texel. They were fairly successful at this task. But other than some physical similarities between the landscapes, there is almost nothing in the film that bears any resemblance to reality.

The opening titles tell the story of Georgian prisoners being taken to Texel, and this sums up pretty much the Soviet propaganda line on the uprising:

> During the war, different groups of Soviet POWs were thrown by fate to many European countries. This is how a battalion of Georgian POWs, gathered from different concentration camps found itself in Holland and was charged by the Germans to work on the construction of embankment defences. The underground Center created in the battalion was in close contact with the Holland Resistance Council. Despite great secrecy, [the] German's distrust of the battalion grew day by day and finally, in order to fully isolate them, the Germans moved the Georgian battalion to the small Dutch island of Texel.[2]

The characters in the film are stereotypes, as was typical of war films produced anywhere in the world at that time. They include a Georgian prisoner who selfishly refuses to take part in the uprising, but later reluctantly becomes a hero. Another is a beautiful blonde Dutch woman who has a bit part conveying a message from the resistance, and who is later seen briefly, submachine gun in hand, blazing away and killing fascists.

The Georgians are tanned, muscular lads, and one or two of the actors later apparently achieved some fame as Soviet sex symbols. The Germans are uniformly small, weak and ugly. In a sense, it's German racism turned on its head. The supermen here are the Georgians, and it is the Germans who are *Untermenschen*.

The film-makers took considerable liberty with the facts. In one entirely made-up scene, a group of young blond Dutch men are about to be hanged by the Germans. But one by one, older members of the community who are watching the hanging step forward to take their places. One of the men – who is not blond – is a Georgian, and he is told that he is not allowed to be replaced. It is a genuinely moving scene, as is an earlier depiction of a hanging on the Dutch mainland.

There's a small sub-plot revolving around a Georgian soldier teaching his language to a German woman. When the rebellion breaks out, the soldier corners the woman and points his rifle at her, but he decides to show mercy and spares her life. This later turns out to have been a mistake, as she is the one who alerts the artillery batteries on the north and south of the island, which remain in German hands, to the uprising – more proof, as if any were needed, that there were no good Germans. Again, this scene has no basis in reality.

Some of the story is designed to suit the Soviet myth that the Georgian rebels were betrayed by the Western Allies. In a dramatic sequence that takes place at night the Georgians are seen removing mines from the sea in order to clear the way for an Allied landing. But despite their efforts, the British never land.

In its essence, the story told by *Crucified Island* is a lie from beginning to end: it shows the Georgians as being prisoners of war, not wearing German uniforms and not carrying weapons. This leads to some highly improbable moments in the plot. How did unarmed prisoners of war get the weapons needed to stage a bloody uprising against the Nazis? In the film, the Germans decide to give some uniforms and some weapons to the Georgians at the last moment, which explains how they are able to begin the rebellion.

It doesn't show how the uprising actually began, with Georgian soldiers slaughtering Germans in their beds, using their razors or bayonets to slit their throats as they slept. That might have been too gruesome, and certainly would not have shown the 'anti-fascist heroes' in a most heroic light.

And yet there are the odd bits of truth which somehow were smuggled into the story. The German commander is shown to be a major, which was the case. The rebellion is timed to break out at 01:00, which is what actually happened. But these are incidental to a story that is almost entirely fiction.

The one true moment in the whole film comes at the very end, with documentary footage of the real Georgian cemetery on Texel and its rows of red roses. It is a jarring moment as it links a fictional story to the reality of what happened on the island.

Remembrance

Over the next few decades the Dutch took a greater interest in the history of the Second World War, creating memorials as well as making films, publishing books and so on. Texel was the subject of some of these, and new memorials appeared on the island, all of them donated by Georgians. One such gift was a new gate to the cemetery made of wrought iron with a copper relief of Saint George slaying a dragon. Even Den Burg's main cemetery in which there are no Georgian graves, but where other Allied soldiers are buried, including airmen shot down over the island, received a Georgian gift. This was a four-metre-high copper 'Tree of Life' which was erected in 1975 and still stands at the entrance to the cemetery. These gifts from Georgia were their way of saying thank you for the help islanders had given to the rebels.

There was increasing interest in the Netherlands in the history of the rebellion on Texel, with several new books appearing and a documentary film, *Sondermeldung Texel*, broadcast on the national television channel in October 1979. Less than two weeks after that film was shown, two Labour members of the Dutch parliament raised the question of the suffering of the islanders who had helped the Georgians, many of whom were showing signs of post-traumatic stress. The parliamentarians argued that Dutch governments during the Cold War had failed to recognise the help the Texelians had given to the rebels. Instead of being praised for their heroism, they were chastised for their sympathy towards 'Russians'. The parliamentarians were echoing Cornelia Boon-Verberg's complaint from the 1960s, when she pointed out that she was more likely to be honoured in Georgia than in her own country.

The reaction of the Dutch government to the Labour members was to have some civil servants look into this, and they found no evidence of trauma among the Texel civilians. However, they learned that little was actually known about the Georgian uprising except on Texel itself, and decided to donate 75,000 guilders to create a permanent exhibition on the island, in a local museum.

Though the Soviet ambassador was allowed to visit Texel each year to participate in the ceremony honouring the anti-fascist fighters of the

Georgian Legion, he faced security restrictions. He and his staff needed to avoid the Dutch naval base in Den Helder. The annual ceremonies continued and the Communist presence grew in importance as we have seen.

The Visit to Georgia

Despite the continuing decline in interest in the rebellion, when the opportunity arose for islanders to visit Georgia in October 1983, more than 200 local people took advantage of this. The trip was organised by the local newspaper, whose editor was very involved with a foundation promoting contacts between Texel and Georgia, and it was designed to allow the Texelians to meet the survivors of the Georgian rebellion.

The islanders were able to travel cheaply to Georgia due to the involvement of a travel agency which specialised in trips to Eastern Bloc countries. That year, about eighty of the Texel veterans were reported still to be alive, and the older Texelians were keen to meet them. Others just wanted the opportunity to visit a country that very few Dutch people had ever seen, especially during the Cold War.

It's been said that some Texelians were hoping to meet their biological fathers. As we noted earlier, there were a number of stories of local women who had relationships with the Georgians. One woman today claims to be the daughter of Loladze. And locals say you can spot who are the children of Georgians, as they look very different from the Dutch children.

The visit went according to the Soviet practice of the time – tightly controlled and supervised. Twenty-nine of the Texel veterans – about a third of those then left alive – came to meet the islanders. The trip was extensively covered in the Dutch media, and the Dutch intelligence service, still wary of the role of the Communist Party in all this, also kept watch.

It may have seemed at the time that Texel had reconciled itself to what had happened nearly forty years earlier, but this was not the case for all the islanders. Theo Witte, whose brother died during the rebellion, said:

Back then, the Georgians chose for themselves. At the very last moment, they wanted to clear their names because they knew that if they didn't do that, they couldn't expect much on their return to Russia. Stalin had ordered them to save the last bullet for themselves. Had they not risen up, we would have been spared from much misery.[3]

Witte was concerned that islanders who had suffered little, whose family members survived the war, had gone off to celebrate with the surviving Georgians.

'I had problems', he said, 'with the fact that the Georgians who survived never recognised ... that they never told people back home what they had caused on the island of Texel.' And he was not alone; others on Texel thought the same way. Some of these wrote letters to the local newspaper expressing that view.

For the islanders who did visit Soviet Georgia in 1983, there were many reasons to go. Time had healed the wounds of war for many. Those islanders who had helped the Georgians during the uprising were growing older, and were keen to see the Georgian survivors while they still could. Because of their advanced age, they no longer feared the secret service treating them as Communist subversives. Anyway, the Cold War was beginning to wind down and there was a massive surge of support for disarmament in the Netherlands and elsewhere in Europe. It has been suggested that another factor was the sense among Texelians that their island was special in some way, and the link to the Georgians was part of that.

In 1985, to mark the fortieth anniversary of the rebellion, seventeen Georgians and seven Russians visited Texel. Six of those were veterans of the uprising. Yet again, they came with a donation for the cemetery. This time it was a commemorative stone with a photograph of Cornelia Boon-Verberg, the 'mother of the Georgians' who had done so much to help them during the war. This was placed in the front of the cemetery near Loladze's grave, and is there to this day.

Events taking place far away from Texel affected how the uprising would be marked in future years. The Berlin Wall came down in 1989.

The Soviet empire began to come apart. After Georgia declared its independence from the USSR in 1991, seventy years after the Red Army had overthrown the elected Social Democratic government there, the commemorations on Texel would not be a Soviet affair but a Georgian one. From this point on, the ceremonies no longer came with the involvement of the Dutch Communists either. Their party had been in steep decline for many years. In fact, the Dutch Communist Party ceased to exist in the very same year that the Soviet Union did, and a year earlier its newspaper *De Waarheid* had closed down.

With the Soviet Union gone, and the Dutch Communist Party just a memory, it seemed as if the annual ceremony at the Georgian cemetery in Texel would also become a thing of the past. Fewer and fewer people came to the annual event at a place which the islanders continued to call the 'Russian cemetery'.

By the time the fiftieth anniversary of the rebellion arrived in 1995, it looked like the annual events would no longer occur. No Russian or Georgian had come for several years. The Dutch had lost interest in marking the event, and focussed their efforts on the official ceremony in Den Burg to commemorate the other victims of the war.

The Georgians buried in their graves on Texel seemed to have been forgotten.

Chapter 17

'A Country of Heroes'

In 1999, Zurab Abashidze, the first Georgian ambassador to the Benelux countries (and indeed, the first ambassador of the newly independent country to *anywhere*) came to mark the anniversary of the rebellion, accompanied by the patriarch of the Georgian Orthodox Church, Ilia II, as well as a large group of religious and civil leaders from Georgia. From that day onwards, the annual ceremony would be a Georgian, not a Soviet affair, with a strong presence from church leaders.

Abashidze apologised to the people of Texel for their losses and suffering. The patriarch led a ceremony in the cemetery in which he announced that 'The Georgian soldiers have defended the Dutch territory against the fascists. Many gave their lives.' It was a surprising continuation of the Soviet line; the Georgians who fought and died on Texel did so as part of the great fight against fascism. They were heroes – no longer Soviet heroes, but Georgian ones.

Part of the story of the Georgian uprising on Texel is the story of their country's struggle to be free from Soviet rule. Some of the politicians and generals who helped create the Georgian Legion – of which the 822nd Battalion was part – did so in the hope that the German invasion of the Soviet Union would result in the liberation of their homeland from Soviet Russian rule. Some of the older men among the exiles had served in the army of the Georgian Democratic Republic until the Red Army invasion in 1921. And among the Georgian émigrés, there was consensus early in the war, both among those who hated the fascists and those who sought ways to work with them, that the Stalin regime would not survive the war. But the regime did survive, and the Georgian Soviet Socialist Republic, as it was then known, lasted for almost half a century following the German invasion of the Soviet Union.

In 1991, as the Soviet Union was collapsing, Georgia had declared its independence. The legal basis for its claim to statehood was the 1918 Declaration of Independence, and initially the constitution of the new Georgian republic was the one adopted in 1921 by the Social Democratic government of the country. Georgia embraced the blood-red flag of the first republic as its national flag, and declared 26 May – the anniversary of the 1918 act of independence – as its national holiday.

Georgian independence in 1991 meant the beginning of a re-thinking of the country's history after some seventy years of Soviet rule. During those decades, the Communist regime imposed a view of Georgian history that erased all memory of the first republic and the Social Democrats who led it. The Social Democrats who had ruled Georgia for the three brief years of its independence were considered to be traitors and pawns of the German and British imperialists. The émigrés in France and Germany were anti-Soviet traitors, as proved by their collaboration with the Nazi regime. The true history of the country was known to only a few, passed on by word of mouth and later by *samizdat* (the clandestine circulation of banned publications).

The process of rethinking the country's history that began in the late 1980s continues today, especially following the centenary of Georgian independence in 2018. Among other things, Georgian historians have begun to revisit the short period of independence in 1918–21, rediscovering the achievements of the Social Democratic government. Part of this process has also been another look at the uprising on Texel. In this we see some new elements that the post-Soviet Georgian state has brought into the picture, but also some surprising continuity with the previous Soviet narrative. For example, both the Soviet regime and the new, non-Communist Georgian leadership were keen to portray the Texel rebels in a favourable light.

On 4 May 2005, to mark the sixtieth anniversary of the uprising, Georgian President Mikheil Saakashvili and his Dutch wife Sandra Roelofs led a delegation to Texel consisting of two veterans of the rebellion, parliamentarians, Patriarch Ilia II, and others. The visit, which had been declared a private one, was extensively covered in both the Dutch and Georgian media. A press release issued before the ceremony said that the Georgian president was honouring those buried in Texel 'as heroes who fought bravely in that war against more than one totalitarian regime', which sums up the official Georgian view succinctly. The Georgians who fought and died on Texel, the press release declared, had 'suffered simultaneously at the hands of Nazi Germany and Stalin's tyranny'. This was the new element in the story: the Georgian rebels on Texel were still heroes, but their heroism consisted of their fight against *both* totalitarian empires, the Communist and the Nazi.[1]

As historian Rob van Ginkel pointed out, 'The idea was that sixty years after the uprising, the Georgian soldiers of the Red Army who turned into the Germans' auxiliaries would at once be de-Nazified, de-socialized and reframed as Georgian heroes – even though some of them had been Stalinist diehards.'[2]

Just before the ceremony, Saakashvili had a meeting with Theo Witte, who had lost his brother during the uprising and was a strong critic of the visit of the islanders to Georgia back in 1983. After hearing Witte's story, Saakashvili dropped the word 'heroes' from the speech he gave in the cemetery. (It was to come back later, as we shall see.)

'It was obvious that some islanders no longer tolerated the fallen Georgian soldiers' heroization,' explained Ginkel. 'If Saakashvili had intended to use his visit to the cemetery for national political purposes he must have been disappointed.' But he got a chance later on.

Two years later, Saakashvili opened a meeting of the Cabinet of Ministers by observing a moment of silence to honour the memory of Pokro Gakharia, one of the last surviving Texel Georgians, who had just died. Saakashvili told his ministers that, in 1945,

> Several hundred armed Georgian fighters disarmed a German garrison and for several months heroically resisted fascist forces. The Georgians fought especially hard and I want to emphasise that they were carrying out a very important mission. However, I must add that their contribution has not been sufficiently appreciated. Many of them were detained and resettled and they endured repressions throughout their lives. Were it not for author Rezo Tabukashvili, Texel would remain a forgotten

episode in Georgia's history. We must not forget that, as Georgia is a country of heroes.[3]

That wasn't the whole story, as Rob van Ginkel has written:

> With tensions between Georgia and Russia mounting, the president apparently deemed it a good moment to point out that the leading force of the Soviet empire had not dealt with its Georgian heroes properly. He carefully avoided mentioning that the Georgians fought on the side of the Germans before the rebellion.[4]

What is striking about Saakashvili's remarks is how much continuity there is between the views of post-Communist Georgia and those of the Stalinist period. The story of the heroic Georgian anti-fascist rebellion – and specifically the reference to Rezo Tabukashvili, who wrote the screenplay for the Soviet film *Crucified Island* – shows the ongoing power of Soviet mythology, which has not been completely abandoned, and instead is now recycled with a nationalist tinge.

This is strange. One of the things that Georgians and others learned under Soviet rule was that the regime could be relied on to falsify history – in other words, you could trust the regime to be untrustworthy. If Stalin and Beria were held up to be heroes (at least for a time), they must have been the opposite. If the Communist regime said that the three years Georgia lived under the rule of the Social Democrats was a terrible time, then clearly something good must have been happening. And so on.

And when the Soviet Communist Party declared that the Georgians on Texel were simply POWs who somehow got their hands on weapons and turned these on the fascists, one might have imagined that post-Communist Georgian leaders would reject this myth too. But they did not do so.

I think this has something do with the nature of the myth itself. All countries have national mythologies and countries that experienced the Second World War have all developed myths about their role in that war. Some of those myths try to build up their histories as being a heroic

A Controversial History

On 11 August 1993, US President Bill Clinton was very pleased to be standing in the Rose Garden of the White House to announce the successor he was proposing to General Colin Powell as Chairman of the Joint Chiefs of Staff, the highest military post in the USA. Clinton's nominee was General John Shalikashvili, a distinguished 57-year-old soldier. Shalikashvili had served thirty-five years in the US Army, including in the Vietnam and Iraq wars. He was the recipient of the Bronze Star Medal with 'V' for valour for his service in Vietnam. He was the first Georgian-American to rise to the top of the American armed forces.

The President was proud of Shalikashvili's life story, from immigrant to America's top general. 'In 1944, when he was 8 years old, his family fled in a cattle car westward to Germany in front of the Soviet advance,' said the President. 'He came to the United States at the age of 16, settled in Peoria, Ill., and learned English from John Wayne movies so that he could take a full course load from his first day in school.'

But within days of the announcement, newspapers were reporting a slightly different take on the general's family history.* General Shalikashvili's father Dmitri, it turned out, also had a military background. Born in 1896, he had served as an officer in the army of independent Georgia. At the time of the Soviet invasion in 1921, he was a Georgian diplomat in Turkey. Once the Georgian forces had been defeated and its government exiled, Dmitri joined other Georgian refugees in Poland, where – like other Georgian officers – he joined the Polish Army. When the Germans invaded Poland, he fought against them. Nothing in this was problematic for his son, then about to be confirmed as the Chairman of the Joint Chiefs of Staff.

---

* Stephen Engelberg, 'General's Father Fought for Nazi Unit', *New York Times*, 28 Aug. 1993, SPN.SP00, http://link.galegroup.com/apps/doc/A174678519/SPN.SP00?u=lonlib&sid=SPN.SP00&xid=8e7de2e8. Accessed 10 May 2018.

But then it transpired that, after the German invasion of the Soviet Union, Dmitri Shalikashvili decided to join the newly formed Georgian Legion. He played a role as a liaison between the Nazi leadership and the Georgians. At some point his unit in the Legion was incorporated into the Waffen-SS – specifically SS-Waffengruppe *Georgien*.

This came out in 1993 shortly after Clinton made the announcement. Dmitri Shalikashvili had written all this down in a memoir, a copy of which was held by the Hoover Institute at Stanford University. The document was discovered by researchers from the Wiesenthal Center in Los Angeles, famous for hunting down Nazis and their collaborators, following a tip-off from a reporter for *Defense Daily*.

Because of the role played by the Waffen-SS in the commission of war crimes across Europe, men who had served in its ranks were not supposed to be admitted to the United States after the war. But Shalikashvili and his family, including young John, were admitted in 1952.

When asked if the Pentagon knew anything about Dmitri Shalikashvili's record in the Second World War, a Defense Department spokesman said that while his service in the Georgian Legion was known, his ties to the Waffen-SS were not. An unnamed 'senior official' from the Defense Department admitted to the *New York Times* that 'The President's moving description on Aug. 11 of his nominee's family origins had been carefully phrased to skirt the issue of the father's service in the German Army.'

Rabbi Marvin Hier of the Wiesenthal Center was quoted as saying that, while still living in Poland, it was clear that Shalikashvili had collaborated with the Nazis. Dmitri's memoir described his unit's transfer to Normandy where it fought against the invading Allied forces after D-Day. After the German defeat in France, Shalikashvili returned to Germany where he was attached to a newly formed Georgian battalion which once again came under the command of the Waffen-SS.

> Shalikashvili's manuscript spoke highly of the SS, according to a *New York Times* report. 'Everything was done with great efficiency,' Shalikashvili wrote, noting that the regular army officers did not appreciate the 'young breed of daring, often quite unorthodox officers of the SS who were keeping pace with changing times'.
>
> Though General John Shalikashvili's appointment was confirmed by the Senate, and he went on to serve with distinction, the revelation about his father's war record led to a number of scholars being called upon to explain the Georgian Legion to an American audience.
>
> One of these, Charles Palm, deputy director of the Hoover Institute, said that Dmitri Shalikashvili was 'a Georgian patriot who sided with the Nazis as an anti-Communist crusade to liberate his native land'. But noted Holocaust historian Raul Hilberg, whose book *The Destruction of the European Jews* is considered authoritative, was more critical. 'No. 1, the man volunteered,' he said. 'Nobody could possibly say he was a draftee. And No. 2, he was in Poland, which meant he had clear knowledge of what the SS and the Nazi regime were all about.'

fight against the Nazis. That is the route the Georgians have taken: they have largely embraced the narrative already given by Artemidze and his comrades back in May 1945. Of course they needn't have done this in order to show that Georgians fought against the Nazis – to do that, all Georgia today needs to do is recognise and honour the memory of the many thousands of Georgians who bravely fought in the Red Army. For example, they could remember Sergeant Meliton Kantaria, one of the two Red Army men who raised the red flag over the ruins of the Reichstag in Berlin in 1945.

But as myths go, the story of the heroes of Texel is not a particularly pernicious one. It could have been much worse, as has been the case in some other post-Soviet republics.

For example, in the Baltic states, there have been some efforts by right-wing nationalists to rehabilitate the memory of local men who volunteered to serve with the Nazis. Each year, on 16 March, Latvian veterans of the Waffen-SS take to the streets in Riga. It is the only march in the world to honour the élite Nazi military unit. Some of the Waffen-SS veterans proudly wear insignia from their old units. Young women on the sidelines hand them flowers. Hundreds of far-right activists march with them, or wave flags to encourage them. At the end of the march, they lay wreaths for their fallen comrades. There are also anti-fascist counter-demonstrators, but those honouring the memory of the Waffen-SS often come in larger numbers.

Nothing like this happens in Georgia today. There are no monuments to honour the men of Hitler's Georgian Legion and there are no parades.

Georgia, like every European country, has its own very small far right. But they are fighting other battles, targeting immigrants and promoting homophobia. They don't care much about the distant past, and certainly not the Second World War.

There are a number of reasons why Georgia has avoided the problem that, for example, Latvia has with its past. One of these is that Georgia had been a part of the Soviet Union for twenty years when the war broke out. Many of the men who served in the Georgian Legion had been born in the Soviet period and had no personal memory of independence. The Latvians, on the other hand, had only briefly been under Soviet rule during the Hitler–Stalin Pact, and many of them welcomed the Germans as liberators when they booted the Red Army out of their country in 1941. The Georgian relationship to the Soviet Union was a more complicated one.

If the men of the 822nd Battalion are remembered at all in Georgia, it is because of their decision to take up arms against the Nazi regime, and the sacrifices they made in the final days of the war.

Chapter 18

Justice

The Nazi regime and its armed forces committed war crimes across Europe. Many of those crimes went unpunished, even when there was no doubt who was responsible. Some of the war criminals survived long after the end of the conflict, leading peaceful lives and never facing justice.

On Texel the German Army committed a series of clearly identified war crimes both before and during the Georgian uprising.

Some weeks before the Georgian uprising 700 civilians – basically, all the men on Texel aged seventeen to thirty-five – were compelled to go over to the Dutch mainland to assist in the construction of German defences. They were returned to the island just in time to witness the Georgian revolt.

While post-war German governments recognised that forced labour was a crime, they refused to pay compensation in many cases. In recent years, the German government explained that Dutch and other forced labourers from across Europe were denied any benefits because though they were *forced* to work in Germany, they were not *detained*. In addition to that, 'Forced labourers from the Western European states were normally not exposed to any racist discrimination and not held prisoner in camps.'[1] As a result, Dutch civilians who were compelled to do war work for the Germans, including many men from Texel, were never offered compensation.

A far more serious crime was the arrest of fourteen Dutch civilians on the first day of the fighting in April 1945, ten of whom were murdered in cold blood by the German forces. The Germans suspected them of supporting the Georgian rebels, but no trial was ever held. On Texel, the authorities erected a monument to honour their memory and local people hold an annual ceremony to remember their sacrifice on the site where they were killed.

Apparently, there was an attempt to convict the island commander Erich Neumann and others of murder in this case. A German court in Oldenburg ruled in 1972 that the crime would have been manslaughter, not murder, but that the statute of limitations meant that the time for bringing the case had expired in 1965. Erich Neumann died peacefully in 1976, never punished for his role in this crime.[2]

Neumann was the principal war criminal on Texel, as Major Klaus Breitner, who had previously commanded hundreds of men in the 822nd Battalion, had lost the vast majority of the troops under his command to the rebel side, and the others had their throats cut. He had no battalion to lead and therefore played little role in crushing the rebellion or with the war crimes associated with that effort. Breitner himself died several years after Neumann.

Far worse in terms of loss of life, was the indiscriminate German bombardment of civilian towns and villages across Texel which began on the first day of the Georgian uprising. Many civilians died on that day and continued to die throughout the month-long fight as German artillery batteries on Texel, at Den Helder, and on the neighbouring island of Vlieland pounded Den Burg and other parts of Texel. Among those killed were a number of children, including children who had come to Texel seeking safety. No effort seems to have been made to spare the unarmed civilian population from the powerful German guns.

The widespread burning of Dutch farms and destruction of property across the island as the German troops hunted down Georgians who were hiding was certainly morally wrong and possibly criminal. In some cases the Germans set barns and other farm buildings ablaze as an alternative to firing their weapons, as we saw in the story of their attack on the group that included Shalva Loladze. The Germans defended themselves by claiming that, as the Georgians were such excellent shots, the only way to ensure that they would not have a chance to kill Germans was to burn down entire farms, smoking the Georgians out or burning them alive.

The crimes committed by German forces on Texel took place in the context of a much broader war crime: the illegal invasion of the

Netherlands, a neutral country, and the occupation of its territory. The German troops on Texel had no legal right to be there and the aggressive war their government unleashed on Europe in 1939 was itself a war crime. As Texel resistance leader Jacob Keijzer put it: 'The Germans had no business being here.'[3]

When the international war crimes tribunal met in Nuremberg, the very first items in the list of charges against the Nazis on trial were conspiracy to commit crimes against peace, and the planning, initiating and waging wars of aggression. In other words, long before the Georgians even arrived on Texel, the German presence on the island was a crime.

While some German war criminals escaped justice because they went into hiding, sometimes even fleeing to South America, the individuals responsible for the war crimes on Texel survived for many decades after the war, their identities known.

Their names do not appear in a book that became known as the 'Nazi Hunter's Bible' – the Central Registry of War Criminals and Security Suspects, which was first published in 1947. This book, known as CROWCASS, lists some 60,000 suspected war criminals, not all of them German and not all of them wanted for specific crimes. In some cases, they were only persons of interest who needed to be interrogated. Adolf Hitler is one of them, wanted for murder in several countries. The list was supposed to be kept secret from the public until 2023, but it was released early by the British government in 2005 and it is now possible to look up the names of those German officers who were responsible for the war crimes committed on Texel.

While there is a long list of Neumanns, none of them was the island commander on Texel. But in the column entitled 'Reason Wanted' one gets a sense of the kinds of war crimes Germans were committing across the continent. For the Neumanns listed there, those crimes include torture, pillage, brutality, murder and 'misc. crimes'.

Major Breitner's name is nowhere to be found.[4]

Chapter 19

An Accounting

Three-quarters of a century after the events, with almost no eyewitnesses left alive, how are we to evaluate the Georgian uprising on Texel? Who was responsible for the more than 3,000 casualties on the island in April–May 1945?

Three candidates have been proposed as being responsible for the tragic events which took place on Texel in 1945: the Georgians, the Dutch Communists, and the Germans.

Many blame the Georgians for the many deaths and the suffering of that time. One of them, Heinz Hlawatschek, who had come to Texel with the German Army and lived there after the war, said: 'I can imagine why the Georgians rebelled; it was a matter of survival. But for Texel it was a disaster. Everyone knew that the war would be over in a couple of weeks and nothing had really happened here in the preceding years of the war. The rebellion was terribly cruel.'[1] Another Texelian told documentary film-makers, 'I had problems with it, because I lost my brother. My biggest problem is the fact that we never got any recognition from Georgia. They never acknowledged how much misery they caused on Texel.'[2]

A woman on Texel summed it up this way: 'I heard they'd said [that] those bastards – if they'd waited another month, Texel wouldn't have been damaged so much. But then they'd [have] been killed at the front.'[3]

Despite their ambivalence regarding the Georgian uprising, most people on Texel still want the Georgians who are buried on their island to be remembered on National Remembrance Day (4 May), though a poll in 2011 showed that 40 per cent disagreed even with that.

The Dutch civilians on Texel were not alone in bemoaning the end of a peaceful occupation due to what was seen as an unnecessary attack on the Germans. British commando raids in the occupied Channel Islands which sometimes led to German retaliation and the punishment of civilians, were often seen as needlessly provocative by the local populations.[4]

While some who have written about the uprising on Texel remain broadly sympathetic to the Georgian rebels, they blame the Communists – both Dutch and Georgian – for deciding to launch the rebellion for their own purposes, showing no concern for the effect on the local population on Texel or on the others who gave their lives. The motivation of Loladze, Artemidze and their comrades was to demonstrate loyalty to Stalin in the hope of preserving their own lives.

But that was not the case for Annie Klein and the Dutch Communists. Instead, they were showing that the Soviet investment in their cause was not without results – and they were compensating in a sense for their behaviour during the first year of the German occupation, when the Dutch Communist Party effectively collaborated with the Nazis. Georgian historian Georges Mamoulia could not have been clearer when he wrote, 'It was the representatives of the Communist Party of Holland, along with Loladze and the other rebel leaders, who are directly responsible for the deaths [on Texel].'[5] Mamoulia was echoing the views of General Maglakelidze, who blamed the Dutch Communists in general and Annie Klein in particular for the tragedy.

During the entire war, he claimed, the Dutch Communists did not fire a single shot at their German occupiers, though they took money from the Soviets to support their underground work. In Maglakelidze's view, these Dutch Communists used the Georgians for their own purposes. He believed that Annie Klein distributed proclamations in the Russian language encouraging the Georgians to rise up, knowing full well that they would be massacred by the Germans who still commanded significant forces in the western part of the Netherlands. Maglakelidze wrote that the Dutch Communists couldn't have cared less about the fate of the Georgians, or the civilians on Texel for that matter.

That was the case against the Georgians and the case against the Communists. But an equally strong argument can be made that it was the Germans who were primarily, and perhaps even solely, responsible for the tragedy on Texel.

Many years after the war, Breitner spoke out publicly about his role and his responsibility for the events that took place on Texel in April 1945. He noted that he had commanded a number of units of Georgian soldiers, including on the Eastern Front. He spoke fondly of how they would – 'in accordance with their eastern mentality' – dream of inviting him to their homes in Georgia after the war. He believed that they were sincere about this.

One of Breitner's jobs was, of course, counter-intelligence. There had been reason enough to worry about the loyalty of the Georgians and the other Eastern Battalions, and there had already been outbreaks of unrest in other parts of Europe. The Georgian troops had been deployed to Western Europe in part to prevent them from being tempted to rejoin the Red Army, as had been happening when they fought on the Eastern Front. There had already been many examples of Georgian soldiers, as well as men from the other Eastern Battalions, switching sides – including the defection of soldiers of the élite Sonderverband *Bergmann*.

More recently, there had been the mutiny of Georgian soldiers near the French town of Hirson, as has already been described. Georgian soldiers had been moved away from Guernsey, some going to the tiny island of Sark, as concern mounted regarding their loyalty to Germany. And in the months running up to April 1945, as we have seen, some of the Georgians in Breitner's unit had already been in contact with the local Dutch resistance, and in particular with Annie Klein and the underground Dutch Communist Party.

Breitner did not seem to have been aware of any of this. Part of the reason for his ignorance is that he relied entirely on his Georgian adjutant Vasil Injia to tell him when disloyal behaviour was discussed among the Georgians. But Injia was having none of this, refusing to play the role of informant, as he preferred to sort out any problems within the Georgian ranks and without involving German officers. Breitner completely trusted his Georgian aide, who he said was even more anti-Communist than the Germans. He believed that the Georgians looked up to him as a father figure, confiding in him. Breitner was convinced that Injia was greatly respected by the other Georgians and could be trusted.

And Injia was telling Breitner that there was no organised Communist Party group among the Georgian soldiers.

In a sense, this may have been true. Though Evgeni Artemidze has often been described at the 'political commissar' within the battalion, and though at the time of the uprising the Georgians were quick to declare their loyalty to the Soviet Union and to Stalin personally (as did the Georgian mutineers in Hirson) this may have been a bit of posturing. There is little evidence that loyalty to Communism and a love of the Soviet leader played much part in the events on Texel.

Injia may well have felt a kind of loyalty to his fellow Georgians and did not want to inform on them. But despite this, when the uprising took place, he was one of the first victims, as the Georgians did not trust him.

The question of what Breitner knew and what he should have known became a subject of debate some years after the war. In 1952, the Swiss historian and journalist J. Torvald wrote a critical book about German policies on the Eastern Front. This triggered an acrimonious debate about the German responsibility – and Major Breitner's in particular – in the run-up to the uprising on Texel.

One of the Georgian émigrés in Germany, Prince Niko Nakashidze, a leader of the Georgian National Organisation in Munich, wrote a blistering attack on Breitner. Nakashidze claimed that Breitner considered 'our compatriots' – meaning the Georgian soldiers under his command – to be second-class human beings. Breitner was said to have said repeatedly that the Georgians were not intelligent enough to serve as officers in the German Army and at best could rise to the rank of corporal. (Loladze and others had been Soviet officers and were given officer rank in the Wehrmacht as well, which Breitner of course would have known.)

According to this account, the German high command was told that Breitner's attitude could potentially lead to a mutiny among the Georgian soldiers. Nakashidze suggested that Breitner should have been removed from his post, and that this had been proposed to the Germans. Because these warnings were ignored, Nakashidze placed the responsibility for the rebellion solely with the Germans.

This view is disputed by others, including Georgian historian Georges Mamoulia. Mamoulia argued that the relationship between the Georgian soldiers and their German officers was actually quite satisfactory for a long time. This had been the case when the battalion was stationed in Poland, and it was the case again when they transferred to the Netherlands. He noted that the Georgians had successfully guarded German railway lines in Poland and Belorussia, defending them against partisan raids.

One German officer, B. Tocha, later made the point that while the Georgians were deployed on the Eastern Front, in the dense forests of Poland, they could easily have run away, but chose not to do so. Other German officers also came forward with additional reports of Georgian loyalty to the Wehrmacht. Colonel Givi Gabliani, one of the top commanders of the Georgian legion,[6] who inspected the 822nd Battalion in December 1943, after the transfer from Poland to the West, noted that both the battalion itself and its commander made a good impression overall. General Köstring, who visited the 822nd Battalion in 1943, considered the Georgian soldiers to be completely reliable.

By mid-1944, the Georgian émigré newspaper *Sakartvelo*, published in Berlin, ran a report claiming that thanks to the efforts of Major Breitner and his faithful Georgian adjutant Injia, the battalion even had a rich cultural life. It said that there were regular weekly talks for the men, including lectures on international affairs and other topics. Some of the men had reportedly volunteered to learn German, which they studied diligently. As Mamoulia concluded, 'Up to the landing of the Allies in Normandy in June 1944, the moral cohesion of Georgian and German military personnel was quite satisfactory.'[7]

But only a few months later, cracks were beginning to show. Following the successful Allied invasion of France and the ongoing Soviet advance toward the German frontier, relationships between Germans and Georgians in the 822nd Battalion began to deteriorate.

In the middle of December 1944, Gabliani made another visit to the battalion, which was at this time still in Zandvoort. (They would move over to Texel the following month.) His report noted a cooling of relations between the Georgians and their German commanders. During his previous visit a year earlier, those relations seemed completely in order. But noticing how bad things had got, Gabliani took the opportunity to give a speech to the battalion staff. He called on the German officers to treat their Georgian brothers-in-arms with respect, tact and sensitivity. He pointed out that the volunteers, including the Georgians, were having a difficult time. The Georgian soldiers, he said, were completely cut off from their families and homes. German soldiers could still return to their loved ones on leave, as Breitner was doing, and communicate with them by post. But not the Georgians. Furthermore, Gabliani told them, don't forget that issues like language were obstacles. The German soldiers, he said, must always remember that they are representatives of the whole German people in their contact with the Georgians.

Around the same time as the Germans were receiving their pep talk encouraging them to treat the Georgians better, those Georgians were trying to persuade the Dutch Communists to support their plan to march on Amsterdam and take on the whole German Army.

Following his visit to the 822nd Battalion, Gabliani returned to Berlin. His message to the headquarters of General Köstring, who was in charge of all the Eastern Battalions, was a clear one: Major Breitner should be moved to another command. There is even evidence of an earlier message from Gabliani to Köstring in October 1944 in which he suggests that one Captain Hinze be designated as Breitner's successor. Either way, months before the Georgian uprising on Texel broke out, some in the German high command had been made aware of possible problems, and the suggestion to remove Major Breitner from the scene had been made.

Some Germans at least were aware of difficulties on Texel. In 1952, Dr G. Kruse of Göttingen, who had served as a translator with the 822nd Battalion, wrote to the historian Torvald about the noticeable deterioration in relations between the Georgian soldiers and their German officers. Kruse was certain that in the final months of the war, there was already fear among the German troops of a possible Georgian insurgency. He told the story of one German corporal who volunteered to serve as a paratrooper in order to get away from Texel. The corporal claimed that, as he had a wife and children, he felt his prospects for survival on the Dutch island were slim if the Georgians rose up and he'd rather take his chances serving with a front-line unit. He was one of those who never returned home from Texel.

Kruse claimed that he learned as early as July 1944 that there was an underground group within the Georgian force consisting of fourteen men. Loladze was their leader, and the group included Melikia and Gongladze. Kruse gave Major Breitner a list of the fourteen names. He suggested that they be arrested and returned to a prisoner of war camp. But Breitner did not take his advice. Instead, Breitner insisted that Kruse provide him with more concrete evidence. This was something Kruse did not have. Instead, he reminded Breitner that there were similar stories of disloyalty among Armenian soldiers stationed nearby, and that those men were disarmed and turned into a labour battalion. Some time later, Breitner acted on Kruse's report, removing two of the Georgians from the battalion ranks – but leaving the leaders, Loladze, Gongladze and Melikia, in their posts. All of those men would go on to play leading roles in the mutiny in April 1945.

In the years following the war, Breitner repeatedly defended his actions and rejected the accusation that he should have seen trouble brewing. In a letter to Torvald in 1952, Breitner responded to the claims made by Kruse and Prince Nakashidze. He denied that conditions for Soviet soldiers held in German prisoner of war camps were inhuman and that this was somehow the cause of the unrest among the Georgians on Texel.

Soviet historians had long claimed that former prisoners of war, like the Georgians of the 822nd Battalion, were forcibly incorporated in the German Army and were not genuine volunteers. In this sense, it was reasonable to expect that in their hearts, they were anti-German and at the right moment they could be expected to rebel. Breitner argued against this, pointing out that most of the Georgians he commanded had been captured not during the early months of the war but only in 1942. This is certainly the case for the Georgian leader, Shalva Loladze, whose plane was shot down in that year. But that was not the case for Valiko Zhgenti, captured in July 1941, or Noe Gongladze, who fell into German hands a month later. Zhgenti and Gongladze wound up on Texel and played leading parts in the rebellion.

According to Breitner, the Georgians were not survivors of the early, improvised German prisoner of war camps in which so many died from hunger, disease and cold. By the time these men fell into German hands, their conditions of detention were far better – and they were kept separate from the Russians. And once in the German Army, they had the same rights as German soldiers and were offered positions of command, including as company commanders. Loladze was one of those who was given commissioned rank in the German Army. From Breitner's point of view, the Georgians had nothing to complain about.

Breitner insisted that he enjoyed working with the Georgians, and that he, like most of the Germans he served with, had invited Georgian comrades to come home with him when he was given leave. Later on, he claimed that this humane policy probably saved his life.

Decades later, in 1979, Breitner was still writing letters defending the job he had done in Texel. He insisted that the reason he survived on the first night of the uprising was the 'love and respect' the Georgian soldiers had felt for him.

Nearly four decades after Operation Barbarossa, Breitner remained convinced that Germany could have won the war against the Soviet Union had it only been more sensitive to the non-Russian minorities, such as the Georgians. His view echoed that of Theodor Oberländer, who created and led the Bergmann Battalion. Breitner believed that the inhumane treatment many Soviet prisoners received was a propaganda win for Stalin. But he insisted that his treatment of the Georgians was anything but inhumane.

Georges Mamoulia summed it up by saying that Breitner obviously bore some responsibility for the revolt taking place. But he was not the only one responsible. It may well be true that Breitner was liked and respected by some of the Georgians he worked most closely with, and that would explain his survival. But there can be little doubt that Breitner underestimated the Georgians and trusted them too much.

The Germans had no business being in Texel in the first place, having launched a war of aggression against the Netherlands in 1940 and illegally occupied the entire country. In the course of that occupation, and particularly during the weeks of the Georgian uprising, the German forces carried out a series of war crimes against both the Georgians and the local Dutch civilian population. Those crimes included taking Dutch men from Texel to do forced labour on the mainland; arresting and murdering ten Dutch men on the first day of the uprising; indiscriminately bombarding civilian population centres; and burning farms and destroying other property as they hunted the Georgians down.

For those reasons, and without denying that there may have been an element of selfishness in the decision of the Georgians to rise up when they did, or that the Dutch Communists played a dangerous game that in the end cost many lives, I still believe that the responsibility for the deaths of Texel remains primarily a German one.

But looking back many decades later, even if we consider the Germans mainly responsible for the tragedy on Texel, how are we to evaluate the behaviour of the Georgians? Until that April night when they took out their bayonets and slit the throats of their German masters, they were considered traitors by the Soviet regime and its Western allies.

Nikolai Tolstoy wrote about a Georgian he knew, whose name he changed to Yashvili:

> In the eyes of Western statesmen and diplomats, Yashvili had become a traitor on that day in Katowice when he volunteered as a recruit for the Georgian Division. But to Stalin, he became one on the day he rode slowly past the weeping old woman and into the arms of the German sentries. To surrender, not to die fighting, was the act of a traitor to the Soviet Motherland, and those in this category were written off as though dead.[8]

Those two decisions made by nearly every Georgian on Texel – first, to surrender to the fascist enemy, and second to don his uniform – were made in order to survive. The alternative in both cases was death, either death in battle or death by starvation or disease in a German POW camp.

The third and final decision the Georgians made after first surrendering to the Germans and then joining their ranks, was to take up arms against them in the final days of the war. And that decision, too, just like others, seems to have been motivated by their desire to survive the war, to come home to the Soviet Union with their heads held high as men who in the end redeemed their honour and did not betray their homeland. For that reason, there's a real consistency between what these men did first in surrendering, then signing up to the Georgian Legion, and then rebelling.

But the question raised by some on Texel, asking if the Georgians were prepared to sacrifice the lives of *others*, of innocent Dutch civilians in order to ensure their own survival is a valid point. Which is why we should ponder what the likely fate of the Georgians would have been had they not rebelled.

The fate of General Vlasov and his men of the Russian Liberation Army may be instructive. Though they too, like the Georgians on Texel, in the end rose up against their German masters, fought against the Waffen-SS, and contributed to the liberation of the Czech capital Prague, they were not spared by the Soviets when they fell into their hands. And the fate of other men who served in the Germans' Eastern Battalions was no better, regardless of whether they attempted to redeem themselves by switching sides in the final weeks of the war.

Knowing this, and knowing that at Yalta the Allies had committed to repatriating any Soviet citizens they found, the Georgians on Texel also knew that they would face a grim fate if they fell into the hands of the Red Army. At the very least, they could expect long prison sentences and forced labour in the camps of the Gulag. They might even be killed, as was the case with Vlasov and many others.

The decision to take on the Germans, to slaughter them in their beds and then to resist fiercely their attempts to re-conquer the island of Texel, was therefore an understandable choice. Those who accuse the Georgians of trying to save themselves are right – but the struggle for survival under the conditions of a world war was a harsh one.

It's true that the Georgians on Texel were first and foremost trying to save their own skins. The alternative was to obey German orders until the end, and go into combat against the British and Canadian armies – something they did not want to do. This too is understandable.

The truth is that the Georgians on Texel did not have *any* good choices.

Much has been made of the fact that the end of the war was near, and any lives lost in these final weeks in April 1945 were entirely avoidable. If only the Georgians had sat it out, it has been said, many hundreds of lives would have been saved. But by the same reasoning, *all* the lives lost in the last days of the war were in vain, as the end result was inevitable and easy to foresee. In the final weeks of the fighting, as the Germans were busy hunting down the last few Georgian survivors on Texel, the war was not peacefully winding down elsewhere in Europe. In some places, it was getting even more horrific, with losses on an almost unimaginable scale.

Three weeks before the war ended, and after the beginning of the Georgian uprising on Texel, the Red Army launched a final ferocious assault on Berlin. Germany was by this point in the war on its knees, utterly defeated, incapable of offensive action. The Nazi regime was in its death agony. The Germans were sending children and old men into battle, many of whom died pointlessly. Even though the war was effectively over, with no possibility of the survival of the Nazi regime, the Red Army launched an all-out attack on the city, which led to an estimated 80,000 Soviet dead and another 280,000 wounded.

In addition to these, German losses in the same battle were estimated at between 92,000 dead and up to five times that number, and the estimated number of civilian casualties in the city was around 125,000. All of those lives – on a scale hundreds of times that of the loss of lives on Texel – could arguably have been saved if the two sides in Berlin had decided not to fight it out when the result of such a battle could easily be foretold.

But that is not how wars end, and that is not how this war ended, not in Texel and not in Berlin.

Epilogue

In the 'Russian Cemetery'

Nearly three-quarters of a century after the uprising, I visited the Begraafplaats Georgiërs – the Georgian Military Cemetery on Texel.

Texel is a small and peaceful island. With a population of just 13,000 people (who are considerably outnumbered by the sheep and lambs), it attracts hundreds of thousands of tourists every year, who come for its beaches, dunes and woodlands. Many of those tourists are Germans.

I walked the two kilometres from the main village of Den Burg down country lanes. In the fields that surround the cemetery, corn grows and sheep graze. Occasionally, a bicycle passes. When I arrived there, on a beautiful late summer day, there were no other visitors. The only sounds were birdsong and the gentle rustling of leaves in the wind.

Today, there are a number of signs and plaques to mark the cemetery but they can't seem to agree on its name. It was at one time called the 'Russian Cemetery' and that is how it is still known to some, though there are no Russians buried there. It is now believed that four of those laid to rest among the Georgians may be North Caucasians, whose battalion had been deployed to Texel before the Georgians arrived, but all the others buried there are soldiers of the 822nd Battalion.

Today, the cemetery bears the name of Shalva Loladze, the commanding officer and leader of the Georgian rebellion. It is maintained by the Dutch Ministry of Defence. And it is now known officially as the Georgian Military Cemetery.

I have visited military cemeteries in other countries, and on other battlefields, but I have never seen anything like this. There are no gravestones, no permanent markers with the names and details of the nearly 500 Georgians buried there. Instead there are a dozen rows of red rose bushes, lined up as if they were soldiers standing on parade.

At the head of the cemetery are a number of symbols, placed at different times and marking the evolution of the memorialisation of the uprising. There's a monument with the symbol of Soviet Georgia, a hammer and sickle, and text in Cyrillic characters. In recent years a large white cross has been erected which was not there in Soviet times.

In one corner of the cemetery, there's a marker with a photo. It's a photo not of a young Georgian soldier, as one might expect, but of an old woman. The woman is Cornelia Boon-Verberg and is inscribed *'van haar georgische zonen'* which means 'from her Georgian sons'. It is dated May 1985, the fortieth anniversary of the rebellion.

At the very front of the cemetery there are three flagpoles. When there are ceremonies, the flags of the Netherlands, Texel and Georgia are flown. The day I was there, there were no flags flying.

On that day, having the cemetery all to myself, I could stroll around, take photographs, sit on a bench and listen to the breeze. There is little to remind one there, in this peaceful and beautiful place, of the horrors that took place in Texel in the spring of 1945.

Appendix

Counting the Losses

No one knows how many people died in the final battle of the Second World War in Europe, which was fought on the island of Texel.

We know with some precision that eighty-nine Dutch civilians died, nearly all of them killed by the Germans.[1]

We also have a good idea of the number of Georgians who were killed. There were about 800 Georgians serving on the island at the outbreak of the rebellion. Of these, 228 survived the conflict, meaning that around 572 died on Texel.

The number of Germans who were killed on the island is much harder to calculate. This is in part due to the fact that many of the German dead and wounded were evacuated from Texel during the fighting. According to Huug Snoek, a member of the Dutch resistance on Texel, hundreds of badly wounded Germans were taken to the mainland on board the ferry *De Voorwaarts*. Men who worked on the ferry told him that the decks were full of German bodies. Overall German losses, including wounded, were estimated by the Canadians at 2,347.[2]

In an interview seventy years later, the last surviving Georgian participant in the Texel uprising, Grisha Baindurashvili, told a journalist that 500 Germans were killed on the first night of the fighting. This is unlikely to be the case as there were only about 400 Germans serving in the 822nd Battalion at that time. But there may have been other Germans killed who were not in the battalion.[3]

On the gravestone of Evgeni Artemidze in Manglisi cemetery – a stone which he designed before his death, and which he proudly showed off to Dutch documentary film-makers – he claimed that the Georgian rebels were responsible for the deaths of 2,500 'Hitlerians' on Texel. This total, too, seems to be an exaggeration and probably includes all the wounded.

Many years after the war ended, bodies continue to turn up from time to time on Texel. It had been assumed that all the German war dead were moved off the island and buried in the Ijsselstein military cemetery near Venray, south-east of Amsterdam. But not all of them made that journey.

One German visiting the island long after the war told of seventeen of his comrades who were buried near the Ongeren bunker complex, just outside Den Burg. Elsewhere, a Texel farmer admitted on his deathbed that he had been forced to bury thirty-three German soldiers in Gerritsland.

Overall, more than 3,000 people died or were wounded in the battle, and probably over three-quarters of those were Germans.

Acknowledgements

Many people helped me research and write this book. Without the support of people in Georgia and the Netherlands in particular this would not have been possible. I'd like to thank the following:

In Georgia, Ambassador Zurab Abashidze, Gulia Artemidze, Lascha Bakradse, Ambassador Jos Douma, Irakli Khvadagiani, Beka Kobakhidze, Rezo Sulava and Davit Turashvili.

In the Netherlands, Arnold van Bruggen (of Prospektor, producers of the documentary film *The Russian War*), Gelein Jansen, Jan Nieuwenhuis (Aeronautical & War Museum, Texel – LOMT), Gerard Timmerman (Hoofdredacteur *Texelse Courant*) and Jasper Wessels (Texel municipal archive).

And elsewhere in the world, Charlotte Alston, Cindy Berman, Derek Blackadder, Kirill Buketov, Roger Darlington, Helen Fry, Donald Graves, Stephen Harris, Janet Johnson, Doerte Letzmann, Georges Mamoulia, Ambassador Stephen Nash, Peter Nasmyth, Roy Nitzberg, Jason Osborn, Clive C. Prothero-Brooks (Royal Canadian Artillery Museum), Donald Rayfield, Sarah Slye, and Bernard Stern.

My publishers in the UK and Georgia – Michael Leventhal and Natalia Alhazishvili – have been much more than publishers, helping to guide the research and writing, and providing encouragement all along the way.

Notes

Prologue

1. There is an account of this event in the *Eastern Daily Press* from 13 April 1962 describing how Dawes and Earl were the first to spot the approaching boat. The clipping was preserved by Earl's family.
2. David Brandon, *East Anglian Coast* (e-book).
3. David Brandon (p. xx) wrote: 'It turned out that the men in the boat were Russian prisoners of war who had appropriated the lifeboat from Texel in Holland and set off pointing towards England, but not before they had purloined a job lot of German officers' uniforms.' In fact the men on the boat were not Russian prisoners, nor were they wearing stolen uniforms.
4. Dick van Reeuwijk, *'Sondermeldung Texel'*, pp. 44–5.
5. Ibid.
6. There is a good account of the Kempton Park facility in Helen Fry, *The London Cage: The Secret History of Britain's World War II Interrogation Centre*, pp. 16–17.

Chapter 1: Georgia and the Georgians

1. Ronald Grigor Suny, *The Making of the Georgian Nation* (London: I.B. Tauris, 1988), p. 193.
2. Donald Rayfield, *Edge of Empires*, p. 327.
3. Cited in Firuz Kazemzadeh, *The Struggle for Transcaucasia 1917–1921* (New York: Philosophical Library, 1951) p. 147. Erich Ludendorff, *Ludendorff's Own Story, August 1914–November 1918* (New York, London: Harper, 1919), Vol. II, p. 302.
4. Leon Trotsky, *Between Red and White: A Study of Some Fundamental Questions of Revolution with Particular Reference to Georgia* (London: Communist Party of Great Britain, n.d.) p. 47.
5. Trotsky, p. 29.
6. Trotsky, p. 28.
7. Trotsky, p. 46.
8. Karl Kautsky, *Georgia: A Social-Democratic Peasant Republic, Impressions and Observations*, Translated by H. J. Stenning and revised by the author (London: International Bookshops, 1921), pp. 88–9.
9. Ibid.
10. Rayfield, p. 329.

11. Georgian National Committee, London, *Georgia and the Georgian Race: Restoration of independent Georgian state after 117 years domination by Russia* (London, 1919), p. 13.
12. Rayfield, p. 330.
13. Kautsky, *Georgia*, p. 89.
14. Rayfield, p. 330.
15. After being out of print for decades, Kautsky's *Georgia: A Social-Democratic Peasant Republic* was recently republished in a trilingual edition – in English, German and Georgian – by Tbilisi State University and the Friedrich Ebert Stiftung, a foundation linked to the German Social Democratic Party.

Chapter 2: Barbarossa

1. Owen Matthews, *An Impeccable Spy: Richard Sorge, Stalin's Master Agent* (London: Bloomsbury, 2019), p. 282.
2. Alexander Dallin, *German Rule in Russia, 1941–1945: A Study of Occupation Policies*, p. 427.
3. Dallin, pp. 414–15.
4. Dallin, p. 415.
5. Dallin, p. 409.
6. Rayfield, p. 358.
7. Rayfield, p. 360.

Chapter 3: The Exiles

1. The source of this story is the testimony of Levi Eligoulashvili, published in the article 'How the Jews of Gruziya in Occupied France were Saved', which appeared in the *Yad Vashem Studies on the European Jewish Catastrophe and Resistance*, VI, Jerusalem 1967. It can be read online at: https://firstrepublicofgeorgia.wordpress.com/category/the-georgian-jews-in-occupied-france/?fbclid=IwAR2mrtGfbh2lOZ8UVXVV2Q4YMeMiazmJhy6Ij-7u26pK0c1COOl9SoalyTo.
2. 'The Righteous Among The Nations –Metreveli Family', Yad Vashem website: http://db.yadvashem.org/righteous/family.html?language=en&itemId=4691757.
3. Rayfield, p. 356.

Chapter 4: Sonderverband *Bergmann*

1. There is one full-length account in English about the Bergmann Battalion: Eduard Abramian and Antonio J. Muñoz, *Forgotten Legion: Sonderverbände Bergmann in World War II, 1941–1945*.
2. Ibid., p. 29.
3. Ibid., p. 27.
4. Dallin, pp. 513–14.
5. Committee for German Unity, *The Truth About Oberländer: Brown Book on the criminal fascist past of Adenauer's minister.*
6. *Truth about Oberländer*, p. 148.

7. Ibid., p. 149.
8. Ibid., p. 151.
9. Ibid.
10. Ibid., p. 148.
11. Abramian, p. 48.
12. Ibid., p. 79.
13. Ibid., p. 46.
14. Ibid., p. 96.
15. Ibid., p. 110.

Chapter 5: Recruiting the Georgians

1. The report of Lomtatidse's interrogation can be found in WO 208/4367 – 'The Georgian Legion'.
2. Van Reeuwijk, p. 18.
3. There is some dispute as to whether Loladze was in fact an officer in the Soviet Air Force; some researchers in Georgia today believe that this was not the case.
4. Interview with Gulia Artemidze, 4 December 2018.
5. Van Reeuwijk, p. 19.
6. Ibid.
7. Ibid., p. 20.
8. WO/208/4367 – 'Notes on Russian Troops in German Service'.
9. WO/208/4367 – SHAEF Intelligence Notes, 6 July 1944.
10. Rayfield, p. 415. He cites Robert Aron, *Histoire des années 40* (Paris, 1976), vol. III, pp. 285, 288.
11. Donald Rayfield, letter to the author, 21 Jan. 2019.

Chapter 6: Unreliable Allies

1. Helmut Heiber and David Glantz (eds), *Hitler and His Generals: Military Conferences 1942–1945* (London: Greenhill Books, 2002), p. 20.
2. Abramian, p. 24.
3. Ibid.
4. PWIS(H)/KP/104. 'Interrogation of Pawawa, Bagrad, Gefr[eiter], 4 June 1944'. Bagrad Pawawa is not a likely Georgian name, but it is what the British interrogators wrote down.
5. PWIS(H)/KP/236.
6. PWIS(H)/KP/191. 'Interrogation of S. Elbakidze – 822 Bn'.
7. This story is based on 'Personal Memories of Some Events During the 1939–1945 War and Activities With the French Resistance Movement' by Christian de Groote, Translated from the French by F. R. de Groote and P. H. Rosher, April 2002, Imperial War Museum, Document 12832, Box Number 03/54/1.
8. Ibid.
9. Matt Rohde, 'A Violent Defection – How a Battalion of Ukrainian SS Troops Mutinied and Joined the French Resistance', *Military History Now*, https://

militaryhistorynow.com/2017/07/30/double-cross-how-a-battalion-of-ukrainian-ss-volunteers-mutinied-and-joined-the-french-underground.

Chapter 7: **Texel in Wartime**

1. *De Russenoorlog.*
2. Ibid.
3. Ibid.
4. Van Reeuwijk, p. 9.
5. Ibid.
6. Ibid., p. 10.
7. Ibid.
8. Ibid.

Chapter 8: **The Georgians and the Dutch**

1. Van Reeuwijk, p. 23.
2. Ibid.
3. Gerhard Hirschfeld, *Nazi Rule and Dutch Collaboration*, p. 111.
4. Van Reeuwijk, p. 24.
5. Ibid.
6. Ibid.
7. Ibid., p. 27.
8. Ibid.
9. *De Russenoorlog.*
10. Ibid.
11. Interview with Gelein Jansen, 5 September 2018.
12. *De Russenoorlog.*
13. Ibid.
14. Ibid.
15. Ibid.
16. Ibid.
17. Ibid.
18. Van Reeuwijk, p. 27.

Chapter 9: **Day of Birth**

1. *De Russenoorlog.*
2. Ibid.
3. Estimates of how many Germans they killed vary considerably. See Appendix: 'Counting the Losses' for a detailed discussion.
4. Van Reeuwijk, p. 39.
5. Ibid., p. 31.
6. Ibid., p. 30.
7. Ibid., p. 34.
8. Ibid., p. 30.

9. Ibid., p. 31.
10. Ibid.
11. Private Papers of H. J. W. Verhoeven, Imperial War Museum, Documents 13710.
12. *De Russenoorlog.*
13. The poster is reprinted in van Reeuwijk, p. 32.
14. Henry van der Zee, *The Hunger Winter*, p. 215.
15. Van Reeuwijk, p. 33.
16. *De Russenoorlog.*
17. Ibid.
18. Ibid.
19. Ibid.
20. Van Reeuwijk, p. 37.

Chapter 10: The German Counter-Attack

1. *De Russenoorlog.*
2. Ibid.
3. Ibid.
4. Fred A. Simon, *A Berliner's Luck: Surviving the Third Reich and World War II*. All the following quotes are from the Kindle edition.
5. Van Reeuwijk, p. 38.
6. Ibid., p. 57.
7. Ibid., p. 43.
8. Ibid.
9. *De Russenoorlog.*
10. WO 208/3629.
11. Ibid.

Chapter 11: Hunters and Hunted

1. *De Russenoorlog.*
2. Ibid.
3. Ibid.
4. Van Reeuwijk, pp. 41–2.
5. *De Russenoorlog.*
6. Ibid.
7. 'The story of Texel uprising as told by its only surviving participant', *Georgian Journal*, 15 May 2015, https://www.georgianjournal.ge/society/30462-the-story-of-texel-uprising-as-told-by-its-only-surviving-participant.html.
8. Van Reeuwijk, p. 46.
9. *De Russenoorlog.*
10. George Mamoulia, *Gruzinskiy legion Vermakhta*. The author is indebted to Natalia Alhazishvili for her assistance in translating the chapter about Texel from Russian to English.
11. *De Russenoorlog.*

12. https://historiek.net/georgische-soldaten-in-leusden-geidentificeerd-na-dna-match/96505/
13. Interview with Gelein Jansen, 5 September 2018.
14. Van Reeuwijk, p. 48.
15. Verhoeven, p. 13.
16. Van Reeuwijk, p. 55.
17. Van Reeuwijk, pp. 55–7.

Chapter 12: Where Were the Allies?

1. HW 1/3687.
2. WO 208/3629.
3. HW 1/3709.
4. HW 1/3721.
5. Terry Copp, *Cinderella Army*, pp. 277–8. His source is the War Diary of II Canadian Corps and Col. Charles C. P. Stacey, *The Victory Campaign: North West Europe, 1944–1945* (Ottawa: Queen's Printer, 1962).

Chapter 13: Liberation

1. Van Reeuwijk, p. 62.
2. Ibid., p. 61.
3. *De Russenoorlog.*
4. T. M. Gavin (ed.), *The Story of 1 Canadian Survey Regiment, RCA, 1939–1945* (Netherlands: Privately printed, 1945), p. 93.
5. 'Veteran Stories: Alex Rezanowich', The Memory Project, http://www.thememoryproject.com/stories/2027:alex-rezanowich.
6. War Diary of 1 Canadian Survey Regiment, RCA – May 1945.
7. Rezanowich, 'Veteran Stories'.
8. De Russenoorlog.
9. Van Reeuwijk, p 61. He should have written 'Tamar' as that is the Georgian version of the name; 'Tamara' is Russian.
10. Murray Campbell, 'The island where Canadians kept fighting', *Globe and Mail*, 7 May 2005, https://www.theglobeandmail.com/news/national/the-island-where-canadians-kept-fighting/article18226617.
11. Lord Tweedsmuir, *Always A Countryman*, p. 312.
12. Ibid.
13. Ibid. As we shall see, Tweedsmuir was misinformed about the fate of the men on their return to the USSR.
14. This text is reprinted in full in van Reeuwijk, p. 58.
15. FO 371/47319.
16. Ibid.

Chapter 14: Back in the USSR

1. De Groote.
2. Rayfield, p. 361.
3. Van Reeuwijk, p. 65.
4. Interview with Jos Douma, Ambassador of the Netherlands in Georgia, 29 November 2018.
5. Lali Papaskiri, 'The story of Texel uprising as told by its only surviving participant', *Georgian Journal*, 15 May 2015, https://www.georgianjournal.ge/society/30462-the-story-of-texel-uprising-as-told-by-its-only-surviving-participant.html.

Chapter 15: The Making of a Myth

1. Interview with Gelein Jansen, 5 September 2018.
2. Van Reeuwijk, p 61.
3. Gilly Carr and Keir Reeves, *Heritage and Memory of War*, p. 98.
4. Ibid., p. 99.
5. Professor Galenson told me this in 1974. Haakon Lie confirmed the story when I met him twenty years later. There is a fuller account in my article 'Stalin's Secret Wars in Norway', available at http://www.labourstart.org/ericlee/norway.html.

Chapter 16: Crucified Island

1. Raspjatyj ostrov (1968) https://www.bfi.org.uk/films-tv-people/4ce2b8d6bc620.
2. The entire film is available on YouTube, but without English subtitles, here: https://www.youtube.com/watch?v=Qe_7YuKxV7A.
3. I am indebted to the essay by Rob van Ginkel, 'Turncoat Heroes or Reckless Egotists? The Ambivalent Memorialization of the "Russian War" on the Dutch Island of Texel', in Carr and Reeves, *Heritage and Memory of War*.

Chapter 17: 'A Country of Heroes'

1. Carr and Reeves, p. 105.
2. Ibid.
3. http://www.saakashviliarchive.info/en/PressOffice/News?p=3529&i=1.
4. Carr and Reeves, pp. 105–6.

Chapter 18: Justice

1. Das Bundesarchiv, Zwangsarbeit im NS-staat, 'Excluded Victims' – https://www.bundesarchiv.de/zwangsarbeit/leistungen/direktleistungen/nicht_beruecksichtigt/index.html.en.
2. Van Reeuwijk, p 37.
3. Ibid., p. 9.
4. Results of search of *CROWCASS – Consolidated Wanted Lists, The Central Registry of War Criminals and Security Suspects* (Uckfield: Naval & Military Press, 2005).

Chapter 19: An Accounting

1. Van Reeuwijk, p 57.
2. *De Russenoorlog.*
3. Ibid.
4. Eric Lee, *Operation Basalt: the British raid on Sark and Hitler's Commando Order* (Stroud: History Press, 2016).
5. Mamoulia, p. 194.
6. Alexander Mikaberidze, *Historical Dictionary of Georgia* (Lanham, Maryland: Rowman & Littlefield, 2nd edn 2015) p. 301.
6. Mamoulia, p. 194.
7. Nikolai Tolstoy, *Victims of Yalta*, p. 36.

Appendix: Counting the Losses

1. Van Reeuwijk, p. 57.
2. The source for this number is the letter from Lt.-Gen. Charles Foulkes, reprinted in full in van Reeuwijk, p. 58.
3. Lali Papaskiri, 'The story of Texel uprising as told by its only surviving participant'.

Bibliography

Archives

Aeronautical & War Museum, Texel, The Netherlands
Artemidze Home, Manglisi, Georgia
Historische vereniging Texel, Texel, The Netherlands
Imperial War Museum, London, UK
National Archives, Kew, UK
The Royal Canadian Artillery Museum, Shilo, Manitoba, Canada

Interviews

Ambassador Zurab Abashidze (Special Representative of the Prime Minister of Georgia for Relations with the Russian Federation)
Gulia Artemidze
Lasha Bakradze (Literature Museum, Tbilisi)
Ambassador Jos Douma (Embassy of the Kingdom of the Netherlands in Georgia and Armenia)
Gelein Jansen (Historische vereniging Texel)
Irakli Khvadagiani (SOVLAB, Tbilisi)
Dr Rezo Sulava (Texel-Georgia Kontact, Tbilisi)

Films

Crucified Island (*Jvartsmuli kundzuli*), directed by Shota Managadze and written by Rezo Tabukashvili, 1968
The Russian War (*De Russenoorlog*), produced by Prospektor, directed by Arnold van Bruggen. 2009

Books

Anon, *The Truth About Oberländer: Brown Book on the criminal fascist past of Adenauer's minister* (Berlin: Committee for German Unity, 1960)
Abramian, Eduard, and Antonio J. Muñoz, *Forgotten Legion: Sonderverbände Bergmann in World War II, 1941–1945* (Bayside, NY: Europa Books, 2007).
Andreyev, Catherine, *Vlasov and the Russian Liberation Movement: Soviet Reality and Emigré Theories* (Cambridge: Cambridge University Press, 1989)

Brandon, David, *East Anglian Coast* (Stroud: Amberley Publishing, 2012)
Carr, Gilly, and Keir Reeves (eds), *Heritage and Memory of War: Responses from Small Islands* (New York: Routledge, 2015)
Copp, Terry, *Cinderella Army: The Canadians in Northwest Europe, 1944–1945* (Toronto: University of Toronto Press, 2006)
Dallin, Alexander, *German Rule in Russia, 1941–1945: A Study of Occupation Policies* (London: Macmillan, 1957)
Fischer, George, *Soviet Opposition to Stalin: A Case Study in World War II* (Cambridge, Mass.: Harvard University Press, 1952)
Fry, Helen, *The London Cage: The Secret History of Britain's World War II Interrogation Centre* (New Haven: Yale University Press, 2017)
Hirschfeld, Gerhard (trans. Louise Wilmot), *Nazi Rule and Dutch Collaboration: The Netherlands under German Occupation, 1940–1945* (Oxford: Berg, 1988)
Lang, David Marshall, *A Modern History of Georgia* (London: Weidenfeld & Nicolson, 1962)
Lee, Eric, *The Experiment: Georgia's Forgotten Revolution, 1918–1921* (London: Zed Books, 2017)
Mamoulia, Georges, *Gruzinskiy legion Vermakhta* (Moscow: Veche, 2011)
Rayfield, Donald, *Edge of Empires: A History of Georgia* (London: Reaktion Books, 2012)
van Reeuwijk, Dick (trans. Judith Hin), *'Sondermeldung Texel': The Georgian Rebellion on Texel* (Texel: Het Open Boek, 2002)
Simon, Fred A., *A Berliner's Luck: Surviving the Third Reich and World War II* (Bloomington, Indiana: Xlibris, 2004)
Tolstoy, Nikolai, *Victims of Yalta* (London: Hodder & Stoughton, 1977)
Tweedsmuir, Lord, *Always a Countryman* (London: Robert Hale, 1953)
van der Zee, Henri Antony, *The Hunger Winter: Occupied Holland, 1944–45* (London: J. Norman & Hobhouse, 1982)

General Index

Bergmann Battalion 35–42
   controversy surrounding 38–40
   defections of troops 41–2, 51
   link to the Georgian Legion 42
Beverwijk, Georgians executed in 115

Canadian Army
   arrival on Texel after VE-Day 127–31
   failure to liberate Texel sooner 131
Crucified Island [film] 157–9, 167

Dutch Communist Party (CPH) 67–72, 145, 149–51, 176–7, 183

Georgia 1–17, 27–34
   Bolsheviks 2, 9–11
   exiles 27–34
      collaborators with the Nazis 32–4
      Social Democratic government in exile 27–8
      NKVD infiltration of 34
      rescue of the Georgian Jews in France 27–32
      rescue of Soviet Jews by Georgians 31–2
   independence (1918–21) 5–17
   independence (1991–) 163–7, 170–1
   province of the Russian empire (1783–1917) 2–4
   relations with Germany during First World War 6–14
   resistance to Soviet rule 17
   Social Democratic Party 2–3, 5, 14–17
   Soviet conquest 17
   visit of international socialist leaders 11, 16
Georgian Legion
   First World War 3–4
   Second World War 43–9
      atrocities 49
      Caucasus 51–2
      desertions 51
      France 53
      Hitler's doubts about 50–1
      morale 178–82
      mutiny in Hirson 53–6
      recruitment 43–9
      repatriation to USSR 132, 136–41, 142–6
      Zandvoort 66–8, 179–80
Georgian uprising on Texel
   airfield 81–2, 100, 102, 107, 113
   Allies informed of mutiny xii, 89, 106–8, 124–6
   attrition, war of 109–26
   beginning of the revolt 83–94
   casualty numbers 189–90
   civilians 82, 87–8, 90–3, 101, 104, 110–11, 115–22
   death of Loladze 115–17
   decision to rise up 80–3
   deployment to Texel 73–78
   escape of Major Breitner 84–6, 97
   execution of prisoners 91, 101, 103–4

German counter-attack 86–7, 95–108
German naval batteries 81–2, 86, 92–3, 95–6, 103
Hitler's reaction to the news 86–7
last victim 122–3
lighthouse 89, 100, 113–14
memorialisation 127, 138, 145, 147–56, 160–1, 175
Oudeschild 81, 88–9, 91–2, 99, 107
plan to seize control of the island 81–2
planned march on Amsterdam 67–8, 73
preparation of the uprising 66–8, 181
redeployment of Georgians to the mainland 79–80
responsibility for 175–85
surrender, German offer of 96
Texla bunker complex 81, 91–2, 94, 98, 100
German invasion of the USSR 18–26
Georgians serving in the Red Army 26
German advance on the Caucasus 25–6
Hitler–Stalin Pact 18–19, 71
surrender and capture of Soviet soldiers 20–4
Stalin's order forbidding surrender 20–1
treatment of German POWs 24
treatment of Soviet POWs 21–4
Vlasov movement (ROA) 133–5, 184
German war crimes 172–4
destruction of property 96, 173
execution of civilians 93, 101, 111–12, 183
failure to punish war criminals 173–4
forced labour and deportations 65, 172, 183
invasion of the Netherlands 61, 173–4, 183

Joan Hodshon [lifeboat] xi, 104–8

Latvia, remembrance of Waffen-SS in 171

Netherlands, German invasion of 62, 127
Norwegian Communist Party (NKP) 150–1

Social Democratic Workers Party (SDAP) 71–2

Texel
annual ceremony to mark the uprising 152–6
description of the island 59
Georgian cemetery 147–9, 151–2, 186–7
German occupation 59–65
Indian soldiers 73
North Caucasian soldiers 73, 186
NSB (Dutch Nazis) 60–1, 90, 101–2
post-war contacts between Texel and Georgia 154–6, 161–2
relations between Georgians and Dutch civilians 75–8
resistance 61, 64, 73–5

Ukrainian Waffen-SS rebellion 57–8

Index of Names

Abashidze, Zurab 164
Adenauer, Konrad 144
Artemidze, Evgeni xv, 37, 44–5, 66–8,
    73–5, 78, 80–2, 88, 104–5, 110, 127,
    144–5, 154–5, 170, 176, 178, 189
Artemidze, Gulia 44

Baindurashvili, Grisha xv, 75–6, 82,
    112, 114, 125–6, 143, 145, 189
Bakker, Jan 105
Balanchivadze, Tina 142
Bentz, Obersturmführer 57
Beria, Lavrenty 17, 25, 167
Bernier, Joe 131
Bondarev, I. 66
Bonne, Marianne 76
Boon-Verberg, Cornelia 74, 89, 116–17,
    152, 155–6, 160, 162, 187
Brasser, Jan 67–8, 75
Breitner, Major Klaus xvi, 46, 79–80,
    82, 84–6, 93, 95–7, 100, 102, 114, 130,
    132, 173–4, 177–8, 180–2
Brimelow, Thomas 140–1
Broekman, Gerrit 93
Buchan, John 132
Buchan, John Norman Stuart (2nd
    Baron Tweedsmuir) 132, 136–7

Catherine II 2
Ciano, Galeazzo 23
Charkviani, Kandid 142
Chavchavadze, Ilya 2
Chkheidze, Karlo 5
Chkhenkeli, Akaki 3, 7–8

Choliashvili, Pido 115
Churchill, Winston 66
Clinton, Bill 168
Crocker, Major C. R. 129

Dawes, Howard xi
de Bloois, Henk 91
de Bloois, Wim 105
de Groote, Christian 53–6, 142
de Waal, Siem 127
Denikin, General Anton 11
Doillon, Simon 57
Doornekamp, Klaas 105
Dros, Cor 105
Ducrocq 53–4
Duinker, Johan 93

Earl, Reg xi
Eelman, Mr and Mrs 111
Eisenhower, Gen. Dwight D. 140, 145
Elbakidze, S. 52
Eligoulashvili, Iosif 28–9
Eligoulashvili, Levi 29
Erekle II (of Kartalinia-Kakhetia) 2

Fletcher, Capt. D. R. 128
Foulkes, Lt.-Gen. Charles 138–40, 145

Gabliani, Givi 36, 179–80
Gakharia, Pokro 166
Galenson, Walter 150
Gavashvili, David 106
Gegechkori, Evgeni 29
Goebbels, Josef 134

INDEX OF NAMES

Goedhart 102
Göring, Hermann 23
Gongladze, Noe 44–5, 81, 84, 102, 113, 143, 155, 181–2
Gugeshashvili, Ivan 31
Gujabidze, Sergei 66, 81
Gviniashvili, Anton 115

Hier, Rabbi Marvin 169
Hilburg, Raul 170
Himmler, Heinrich 17, 23
Hindenburg, Field Marshal Paul von 7
Hinze, Captain 180
Hitler, Adolf 18, 23, 50, 86–7, 114
Hlawatschek, Heinz xvi, 62, 175
Holba, Major Lev 57
Hooijberg, Remmert 105
Huysmans, Camille 16

Ilia II, Patriarch 165
Ilyasov 42
Injia, Vasil 177–9

Kacharava, Vladick 54, 56
Kantaria, Meliton 26, 170
Karkashadze, Simon 106
Kautsky, Karl 1, 14, 16
Keijzer, Jacob xvi, 61, 64, 73–4, 78, 82, 88, 92, 121–2, 130, 174
Keijzer, Piet 93
Keijzer, Wim 93
Kelder, Wim 61, 88, 104, 152
Kerensky, Alexander 5
Kerselidze, Leo 4, 32–3
Khuberaishvili, Col. 143
Kirk, Lt.-Col. William Douglas xvi, 128–30
Klein, Annie (Annie van Ommeren-Averink) 67, 72–3, 75, 80, 152, 176–7
Knol, Jaap 105
Köstring, General 48, 179–80
Kooger, Marinus 105
Kress von Kressenstein, Freiherr Friedrich 7, 10, 13–14

Kruse, Dr G. 180–1
Kurashvili, Col. 143
Kuseleff, Hauptmann 46
Kvinitadze, General Giorgi 45
Kutsenbach, Baron Walter von 38

Lenin, Vladimir Ilyich 3, 5, 14–16, 71
Lie, Haakon 150–1
Loladze, Shalva xv, 44–5, 66–8, 76, 80–1, 84, 90–2, 94, 96, 104, 106, 108, 115–16, 138, 145, 148, 152–3, 156, 161, 173, 176, 178, 181, 186
Lomidze, Varlam 45, 122–3
Lomtatidse, Oberleutnant 43, 45, 48, 51–2
Lossow, General Otto von 7
Ludendorff, General Erich 6–7

MacDonald, James Ramsay 16
Machts, Col. 48
Maglakelidze, General Shalva xvi, 33–4, 47, 52, 133, 144, 176
Mamiev, Michail 52
Mamoulia, Georges 176, 179, 182
Managadze, Shota 157
Marquet, Adrian 16, 28–9
Matchaidze, Akaki 81, 99, 103, 106
Melikia 81, 92, 181
Metreveli, Sergei 31
Montgomery, Field Marshal Bernard 79, 124, 126
Mussert, Anton 61

Nakashidze, Niko 178–9, 181
Neumann, Erich 173–4
Nikuradze, Alexander 33
Nozadze 81

Oberländer, Dr Theodor xvi, 37–40, 42, 182
Okropiridze, Shaliko 36
Oremus, Jos 93

Palm, Charles 170

Pen, Andries 93
Pen, Herman 93
Pieper, Theo 92–3
Plekhanov, Georgi 3
Powell, General Colin 168

Rabinovich, Arkadi 31
Ramishvili, Noe 8
Rayfield, Donald 6, 12, 14, 49, 142
Reviashvili, Georgi 106
Rezanowich, Alex 128–31
Röhren, Dieter 45
Roelofs, Sandra 165
Roeper, Jan 90
Roosevelt, Franklin D. 17
Rosenberg, Alfred 22, 33
Ruimers, Piet 93

Saakashvili, Mikheil 165–7
Schliephack, Horst 4
Shalikashvili, Dmitri 168–70
Shalikashvili, General John 168–70
Shamil, Seid 33
Shaw, Tom 16
Simon, Fred Adolf 97–8, 100–1
Simonds, Lt.-Gen. Guy 126
Smit, Leo 65
Smit, Theo 122–3
Snoek, Cor 61, 82
Snoek, Huug 61, 82, 83, 101, 189
Snowden, Ethel 16
Solzhenitsyn, Alexander 155
Sorge, Richard 18
Stalin, Iosif 2–3, 10, 16, 18–21, 25, 36, 142, 144, 147, 167
Stalin, Yakov 49

Tabukashvili, Rezo 157, 166–7

Teuwsen, Johnny 83, 84
Tocha, B. 179
Tolstoy, Nikolai 183
Torvald, J. 178, 180
Trotsky, Leon 5, 8–11
Tsereteli, Irakli 5
Tsereteli, Prince Mikheil 32–3
Tsiklauri, Lt. 36

van der Kooij, Klaas 105–6
van der Linden, Captain Piet 62
Vandervelde, Emil 16
Veening, Dr 101, 123
Verhoeven, Hans xvi, 59, 77, 87, 117–21
Vlaming, Piet 101–3
Vlasov, Lt.-Gen. Andrey Andreyevich 49, 133–5, 145–7, 152, 184
von der Schulenburg, Count Friedrich Werner 4, 47

Westdorp, Jaap 105
Wilhelm II, Kaiser 8
Wilhelmina of the Netherlands, Queen xii, 62
Witte, Jan 93
Witte, Kees 93
Witte, Theo 161–2, 166

Yashvili 183
Yegorov, Mikhail A. 26

Zegel, Melle 111–12
Zhgenti, Valiko 44, 83, 182
Zhordania, Noe 3, 5, 10–11, 29
Zigel, Emil 31–2
Zuganov, Asis 40
Zwaard, Tom 65